That so many ski areas have evolved in Colorado—more than 35 and counting, including 14 that may be considered truly major in scope—is the culmination of factors of climate, geography, and vision. Add to this a splash of history, a dash of money, and some of that inexplicable quality of star appeal that visits some places before others, and the picture is complete.

ROD WALKER/THE STOCK BROKER

Skiers choose Colorado above all other states. Nearly one in five lift tickets issued in the entire country is sold here. Vail is both the nation's largest and most popular resort. Seven Colorado areas rank among the top ten in the U.S., which are Vail; Mammoth, California; Killington, Vermont; Steamboat; Keystone; Breckenridge; Winter Park; Snowmass; Heavenly Valley, California; and Copper Mountain. More skiers visit the Ski the Summit quartet of Breckenridge, Keystone, Copper Mountain, and Arapahoe Basin than all of Utah.

COLORADO**SKI**COUNTRY

Charlie Meyers Number Four

DAVID LOKEY/VAIL-BEAVER CREEK

Each year between $50 million and $80 million is invested on such mountain improvements as lifts, trails, and equipment. Add to this expenditures for condominiums, lodges, restaurants, and all the other trappings of the sport, and the sum soars into the billions.

By best estimate, skiing adds $1.3 billion to the Colorado economy each year, exceeded only by agriculture as an income source. It is a crop which requires no price supports and is not in danger of being undercut by foreign competition.

DAVID HISER/PHOTOGRAPHERS ASPEN

Colorado Geographic Series Staff

Publishers: Michael S. Sample,
 Bill Schneider
Editor: Marnie Hagmann
Photo editor: Jeri Walton
Design: DD Dowden
Graphics: DD Dowden
Marketing director: Kelly Simmons

Front cover photo

Bruce Benedict/The Stock Broker.

Back cover photos

Left, Robin B. Smith/Aspen Skiing Company/Colorado Ski Country USA; right, David Lokey/ Vail-Beaver Creek.

Copyright © 1987 by Falcon Press Publishing Co., Inc., Helena and Billings, Montana.

Library of Congress Number: 86-82747
ISBN: 0-937959-16-2 (softcover)
ISBN: 0-937959-17-0 (hardcover)

Design, typesetting, and other prepress work by Falcon Press, Helena, Montana.

Printed in Hong Kong.

That all this happened in a relatively wild place, more than a thousand miles from major population centers, also is the result of happenstance and intrigue. There are a thousand stories beneath the twinkle and glitter of Colorado Ski Country. To find some, one must dig back through the bones and rust of a century or more.

Major
ski
areas

N

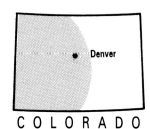

C O L O R A D O

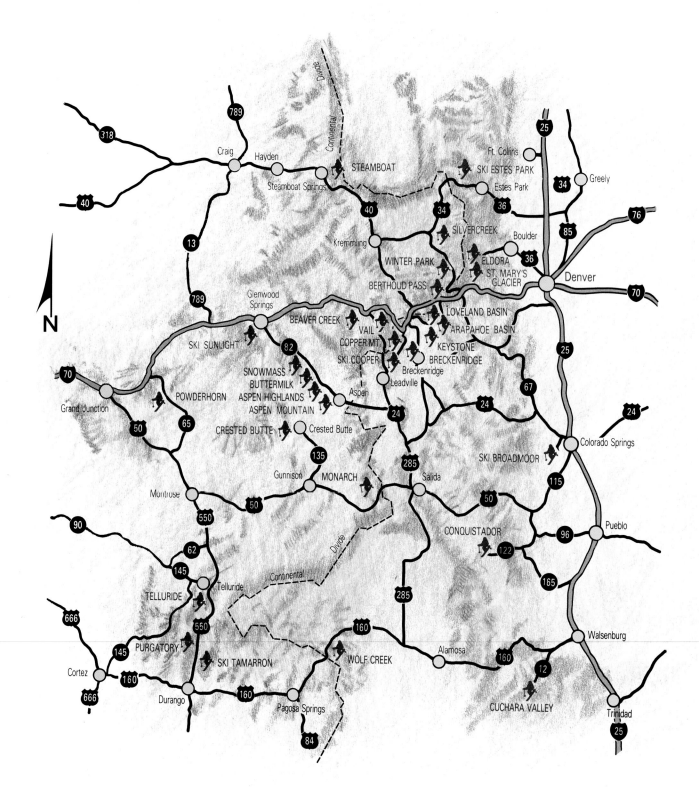

Denver

318

789

40

13

789

25

34

36

76

85

36

70

Craig Hayden

Steamboat Springs

STEAMBOAT

Ft. Collins

SKI ESTES PARK

Estes Park

Greely

40

Kremmling

34

SILVERCREEK

WINTER PARK

BERTHOUD PASS

Boulder

ELDORA

ST. MARY'S
GLACIER

Denver

Glenwood
Springs

BEAVER CREEK

LOVELAND BASIN

ARAPAHOE BASIN

SKI SUNLIGHT

82

VAIL

COPPER MT.

SKI COOPER

KEYSTONE

BRECKENRIDGE

Breckenridge

POWDERHORN

SNOWMASS
BUTTERMILK
ASPEN HIGHLANDS
ASPEN MOUNTAIN

Aspen

Leadville

70

Grand Junction

50

65

CRESTED BUTTE

Crested Butte

24

24

24

67

Colorado Springs

135

SKI BROADMOOR

Montrose

550

50

Gunnison

MONARCH

285

Salida

50

115

Pueblo

90

62

145

CONQUISTADOR

122

96

165

Telluride

TELLURIDE

Continental

Divide

285

Walsenburg

666

145

550

PURGATORY

SKI TAMARRON

160

Alamosa

160

160

12

Cortez

160

WOLF CREEK

666

Durango

160

Pagosa Springs

CUCHARA VALLEY

Trinidad

84

25

Contents

A path to somewhere 8

Echoes of a high old time 12

All the fixings 22

The best and brightest 30

   Vail, a giant on the prowl
     Vail Mountain - Beaver Creek, the crown prince
   Aspen, queen of the Rockies
     Aspen Mountain - Snowmass, a family affair -
     Aspen Highlands, a well-kept secret
   Steamboat Springs, Ski Town, U.S.A.
   Winter Park, the light at the end of the tunnel
   Ski the Summit
     The Kingdom of Breckenridge - Keystone,
     perfection in the pines - Arapahoe Basin, a natural
     high - Copper Mountain, skiing above all
   Stirrings in the southwest
     The Butte is a beaut - Telluride: wild, woolly, and
     wonderful - Purgatory, a solace for lost souls

   In praise of all things small

A new day for the old way 82

Back to the future 92

A path to somewhere

The Tenth Mountain Trail

It is a trail which has a beginning but no end, it connects nothing more tangible than dreams, and its direction leads straight to the stars.

The name, Tenth Mountain Trail, means little to anyone whose heart does not leap at the sight of great shining peaks and the faint whisper of skis against snow. The prospectus for this long and winding path through the winterscape of the central Colorado Rockies suggests that it connects the world-famous ski resorts of Aspen and Vail, which it as yet does not.

It is entirely possible, even plausible, to forge boldly forth with heavy pack and cross-country skis from the very heart of Aspen, risking the superior stares of fur-clad tourists. But it requires a leap of faith and a bound across a major highway to reach Vail on the other end. In truth, trail's end comes in an empty valley called Yeoman Park, 20 miles southeast of the hamlet of Eagle, a full 30 miles and light years from Vail. It is a bit closer to Beaver Creek, Vail's precocious progeny, but to get there by the most direct route through a dense tangle of wilderness might tax even the determination and skills of those crusty old soldiers of the Tenth Mountain Division for whom the route is named.

All this is merely fragmented geography. The Tenth Mountain Trail does not join Aspen and Vail so much as it connects

► *A cornice crowns a tempting swatch of untracked snow in China Bowl, part of the vast expanse on the back side of Vail.*

DAVID LOKEY/VAIL-BEAVER CREEK

► *Fresh snow on evergreens, tall peaks glistening white. This is the magic of mountains in winter.* ANNIE GRIFFITHS/WEST LIGHT

► *If immersion is, indeed, an element of rebirth, then there may be more to this thing called powder skiing than anyone could have imagined. The scene is from Winter Park.* ROD WALKER/ WINTER PARK

the very fabric of Colorado skiing—past, present, and future. It is only fitting that it originates from the antique charm of Aspen, that citadel of Victorian splendor which emerged more than 40 years ago as the first, and grandest, ski resort in all the Rockies. And it is equally appropriate that the intrepid tourer, albeit with auto-shuttle assist, ends up amid the beguiling glitter and glamor of Vail, that Johnny-come-later which more recently has usurped the title of biggest and, perhaps, best.

It was the famed architect Frederick ''Fritz'' Benedict of Aspen, a Tenth Mountain veteran, who became the driving force for this historic link. Benedict's notion was to carve his path on the most direct route between the two resorts, a course which would come straight into the backside of Vail on a high route through the wilderness. But there is danger here, steep terrain with a propensity for avalanche and beyond the ability of most skiers. Realizing this, Benedict then directed his route substantially to the north and west—nowhere near Vail.

There is some talk of leaping the trail across Interstate 70 and bringing it back towards Vail from the north. But it is equally probable that before the trail gets to Vail, Vail instead will come to it. Such is the present direction of Colorado's ski industry: expansionist, aggressive, soaring into the clouds. One day soon, Vail may become the largest ski resort in the world, and a seemingly endless web of lifts and trails and lodges might extend along that highway corridor as far as the eye can see or the mind imagine.

But before straying too deeply into skiing's growing maze, slip ever so softly back into a velvet yesterday, a purer time when the horizon of skiing was bounded only by rich imagination. ■

▶ *It's flying. It's freedom. It's a hotdogger at Vail who has found a camera close by.*
DAVID LOKEY/VAIL-BEAVER CREEK

Echoes of a high old time

The history of Colorado's ski industry

Now, as in the past, skiing follows gold. There is some debate as to when and where, but one thing is certain: Colorado's first skiers were miners of Scandinavian descent, hardy pioneers who clung tightly to the customs of the old country and for whom "Norwegian snowshoes"—skis up to 12 feet long— were as much a part of life as the musings of Ibsen or the melodies of Grieg. It is somewhat less difficult to pinpoint the first competitions, most likely in the Crested Butte area at a mining camp called Irwin in 1883. The existence of a racing club at Crested Butte in 1886 has been documented, as have regular competitions between the miners of that district and the "flatlanders" from down the valley in Gunnison.

It was this time and place which provided one of skiing's grander episodes, that of Albert Johnson, a ne'er-do-well prospector by way of Canada who abandoned his failing mining career to carry mail on skis over what is now Schofield Pass, a brutal route from the camp of Gothic near Crested Butte across a high divide to Crystal.

Johnson's professional activities quite naturally made him one of the best racers of the day, and his exploits are an enduring part of local lore. Legend has it that Johnson was the loser in Colorado's first recorded ski race, a straight schuss down a steep mountainside won by a brash teenager named Charlie Baney, who, by accident or design, dropped into a tuck and sped past the startled Johnson at the finish. An amusing, if not factual, sequel to this event is that under the guise of friendship and congratulation, older miners filled young Baney with whiskey

at a subsequent race, assuring that he no longer would be a threat.

At about the same time, Swedish miners were schussing the slopes near Aspen, and down in the southwest, at Ouray, the Mount Sneffels Snowshoe Club was establishing a tradition for which later generations of Colorado skiers have been grateful. It was not so much what the Sneffels gang achieved during the races that made it famous as what happened afterwards. These were the first party lizards of Colorado ski lore, and their legendary capacity for imbibing has served as a benchmark for après-ski revelers ever since.

Although skiing was well established in virtually every mountain enclave by the turn of the century, it remained for a latter-day Norwegian emigrant, a stonemason named Carl Howelsen, to

▶ *Ski pioneer Carl Howelsen, standing second from left, poses with the other members of the Scandinavian jumping team, right.* COURTESY, COLORADO HISTORICAL SOCIETY F-8083

▶ *Women skiers at Breckenridge in 1889, far right.* COURTESY, COLORADO HISTORICAL SOCIETY F-8277

give it a real impetus and definition. With evangelical zeal and a stuntman's skill, Howelsen blazed a trail during the teens and early twenties which began in Denver, wandered north and west through the Grand Valley to Hot Sulphur Springs, and ended in Steamboat Springs, where the ski fires since have burned white-hot for three-quarters of a century. It was Howelsen, too, who fanned the passions of Denverites. Flames of enthusiasm leaped up to the snowfields on high passes like Berthoud and Loveland and prompted a visionary named George Cranmer to start an official Denver city playground at a place where trains poked their sooty heads through the west portal of the new Moffat Tunnel under the Continental Divide. With more precision than pretense, it was called, simply, Winter Park.

At about the same time, similar developments were popping up all across the mountains. At no place did this occur with more serendipity than at Aspen, where for better or worse, things often do not turn out as intended. Tom Flynn, a Roaring Fork valley pioneer, Billy Fiske, an Olympic bobsled champion, and Ted Ryan, an investor, joined forces in 1936 to hire famed Swiss avalanche expert Andre Roch to survey a planned ski resort. The site was Mount Hayden, an imposing mountain with steep flanks near the old mining town of Ashcroft, a dozen miles up the Castle Creek valley.

But when money was not forthcoming for the Hayden project, Roch settled in to teach skiers of the Roaring Fork Winter Sports Club. He took his skiers on the big mountain called Ajax towering above the sleepy town of Aspen, where the doldrums of a half century without mining had dropped the price of a house lot to $5. The market was not brisk. Roch

laid out the historic run on Ajax which bears his name, and a small band of enthusiasts strung up a boat tow, a ponderous ten-passenger sled-like device with wooden railings pulled uphill by an old mining cable and a gasoline motor. Skiing at Aspen had begun.

It is a terrible irony that Fiske soon became the first American pilot to lose his life in World War II, and Flynn, chagrined,

abandoned his project. Mount Hayden today remains as enchanting—and pristine—as ever, untouched by skis, save an occasional assault by a few backcountry powder hounds, and no closer to development than on that day Roch arrived more than a half-century ago.

Those ancient rumblings began stirring again in the Crested Butte area, where abandoned mine cables were improvised

► *Backcountry skiers climb to conquer, a common sight above timberline on Independence Pass near Aspen.* DAVID HISER/PHOTOGRAPHERS ASPEN

Carl Howelsen, father of Colorado skiing

Johnny Appleseed only planted apples.

What Carl Howelsen sowed across the mountains of Colorado has far more lasting value, both for the spirit and the economy. Travelling from place to place, much like the legendary apple man, the "Flying Norseman" carried the message of skiing to mountain communities throughout the northern part of the state, winning hearts and awakening the land from its frozen slumber. When he was done, no one he touched would ever view winter in quite the same way.

A surprising amount is known about the early years of a man born a shoemaker's son in 1877, much of it from a loving biography prepared by his son Leif, himself a frequent visitor to Colorado in recent years. Howelsen's talent for skiing in the Nordic style surfaced early, and in both 1902 and 1903 he won the 50-kilometer race at the Holmenkollen, the most important ski race in the world at that time.

But the feet which skied so fast also had wanderlust, and pushed by hard times, he took his bricklayer's skills to America, stopping finally in 1905 at Chicago, a gathering place for Norwegian immigrants. That very winter, he founded the Norse Ski Club of Chicago, built a ski jump, staged the first ski competition in that city, and got his picture in the *Daily Tribune*. It also was in Chicago that Howelsen took another bold step. On his first union card, he Anglicized his name from its original Karl Hovelsen.

His skill and daring in ski jumping also caught the attention of the Barnum & Bailey Circus, which paid Howelsen the extravagant sum of $200 a week to perform to rave reviews in such places as Madison Square Garden. He also received offers to perform as far away as England—heady stuff for a small, quiet man with chiseled features and a broad mustache.

Howelsen heard stories of a far-off place with towering mountains and deep snow called Colorado, and in 1909 he hopped a train to Denver. It would be grossly inaccurate to suggest that Howelsen introduced skiing to Colorado. What he did was serve as a catalyst to bring a smoldering interest to a peak of excitement wherever he went. Howelsen had learned enough showmanship at the circus to know how to rally a crowd. When he gave a ski exhibition, the whole town turned out.

Howelsen's first performance at Hot Sulphur Springs, a small ranching community in the Grand Valley, was so successful that word traveled quickly back to Denver, which then began to push for its own carnival. By 1913, a club had been organized and skiing was an established part of the winter sports scene. A year later, 20,000 spectators witnessed a Howelsen jump at Inspiration Point on the western rim of the city. It was a different kind of inspiration which gave Howelsen a more enduring niche in Denver ski history. Spurred by the Norseman's feats, George Cranmer, later to become director of parks and improvements, became infatuated with the sport, and this personal interest was the mainspring for the establishment of Winter Park as a city-owned ski center.

But it was not until he was persuaded to visit Steamboat Springs, a sleepy ranching town in the north-west corner of the state, that Howelsen's growing romance with Colorado became complete. Where wide valleys nestled among broad-shouldered peaks, Howelsen found the place that he would call home.

In 1921, at the athletically advanced age of 44, Howelsen won the National Professional Ski Jumping Championships in Denver. Later that fall, he suddenly decided to travel to Norway, to visit the "Old Country." Nobody could have imagined he would never return.

The Howelsen legacy has endured as few before or since. In almost every ski resort in the state there are echoes of the quiet enthusiasm of this remarkable man, the father of Colorado skiing.

► *Carl Howelsen, the "flying Norseman."* COURTESY, COLORADO HISTORICAL SOCIETY DETAIL F-8083

► *Spectacular Hallett Peak frames Tyndall Gorge in Rocky Mountain National Park, a favorite of ski tourers.*
NATIONAL PARK SERVICE
PHOTO BY MICHAEL SMITHSON

in 1939 into the state's first chair lift, forming a ski area called, appropriately, Pioneer. But the U.S. Forest Service deemed the site hazardous, and the operation was shifted to Rozman Hill in Crested Butte, setting the stage for the modern resort two decades later.

While dramatic and historic, these enterprises scarcely were rare. Other ski sites began popping up all across Colorado's mountain expanse like mushrooms after a spring rain. There were trails at Monarch Pass, Wolf Creek Pass, Lake Eldora, St. Mary's Glacier, and Estes Park—all of which have lifts today—as well as at Glenwood Springs, Creede, Hoosier Pass, Green Mountain Falls, Homewood Park, and a dozen other places where skiing has faded with time.

The year was not yet 1940, and there was a world war yet to fight.

Colorado's ski troops

It was a stunning, almost unbelievable sight. Buildings stacked row upon row. Men and machinery milling about. Smoke hanging like a shroud in the thin, cold air at an elevation of 9,200 feet.

Any motorist churning up Highway 24 toward Tennessee Pass in Colorado's central Rockies during the early forties was struck by the sight of Camp Hale, the home of America's ski troops, the Tenth

The order of the cross

It is race day at a Colorado resort, a sun-streaked morning marked by high spirits and keen competition among the several dozen strong young men competing for considerable glory and a small sum of cash on a satellite professional tour. This is racing in its most exciting form, two skiers straining side by side down two parallel and nearly identical courses. In its most sublime expression, the two descend like marionettes in a perfectly choreographed dance through a thicket of colorful control gates, ending in a mad dash to the finish in which only hundredths of seconds determine the winner.

Suddenly there is something terribly wrong. One racer loses his balance, spins out of control, and a ski windmills into the head of his opponent. What moments earlier had been drama now is disaster. A call goes out and within seconds a skier appears wearing the white cross which marks him as a ski patrolman. Moments later there is another, and another. With skill born of long hours of training and years of experience, they work feverishly over the stricken man, stanching the flow of blood, keeping him alive until an emergency helicopter whisks him away to a Denver hospital. Mirac-

ulously, the racer lives.

This is but a dramatic example of a scene repeated in varying forms several times each day at any major ski area. This is the work of the ski patrol, a band of free spirits who are at once the hardest-skiing mavericks on the mountain and every skier's link to survival.

Ski patrolmen always have seemed larger than life. They are the people who have complete command of skiing's most contested territory, the lift line. If they choose, they ski every day and are paid for it. They get to the powder before anyone else, and when day is done, gather in tight clusters in a slopeside tavern to relate deeds of derring-do of which more mortal skiers can only dream.

Yet beneath this swashbuckling exterior with the distinctive cross on the back of the parka is a highly trained and regimented professional who is a qualified emergency medical technician, is skilled in the mechanical aspects of several forms of rescue, and should the occasion arise in some extreme emergency, is obliged to risk his life to save yours.

These are the people who open the ski area in the morning, close it with a meticulous sweep in the afternoon, and should someone request it, go long into the night in search of a missing skier who almost invariably turns up hours later at a local watering hole, completely unaware that he ever was lost in the

first place.

Patrolmen deliver explosive charges which bring down avalanches, employ ropes and slings to liberate anxious skiers from stalled lifts, and occasionally haul seriously injured skiers downhill by toboggan. But mostly they help people with things like broken equipment, retrieve possessions lost from lifts, or chastise some miscreant skiing out of control.

They are the eyes and ears of a ski resort, safety officers ever on the lookout for a danger spot to be roped off or a problem to be monitored. At the larger resorts, they may employ a computer to ac cumulate data on types of accidents or precise locations on trails to facilitate corrective action.

There are two kinds of patrolmen. Members of the professional patrol are full-time salaried employees of the resort. Their ranks may be augmented by the National Ski Patrol, volunteers who serve part-time on a predetermined schedule, generally on weekends when expanded crowds demand more supervision. Recently, larger resorts have gone almost exclusively to professionals, while smaller areas that receive a large infusion of weekend skiers rely more heavily on volunteers.

When the phone rings up in the patrol shack, they are all the same, quick to respond, always mindful that the next call could save a life. For all that, they more than earn that first crack at the powder.

BRECKENRIDGE SKI AREA

► Mountain rescue work can have its trials, as this Aspen volunteer discovered in a bout with a snowstorm.

DAVID HISER/PHOTOGRAPHERS ASPEN

Mountain Division.

In one of the most compelling stories of World War II, this band of hastily assembled and often misdirected men from every corner of the country played a telling role in the downfall of Germany's Third Reich. And, beyond that, they virtually laid the foundation for America's ski industry.

Apart from a few isolated conflicts in Europe, winter combat on skis was little known and less understood by the rest of the world. Then in 1939 a woefully undermanned band of Finns using lightweight, mobile skis kept a substantial portion of the Russian army at bay for months. Suddenly, the world took note.

Still, it was not until a Greenwich, Connecticut, insurance broker named Charles Minot "Minnie" Dole managed to stir a slumbering War Department in 1940 that the United States caught the drift. Dole was no ordinary businessman. At a time when the sport was in its infancy, he had been skiing for years over various parts of New England. Dole also was a man of action. Two years earlier, after a friend was killed in a skiing accident, he founded the National Ski Patrol with the hope that prompt and highly trained assistance might prevent such mishaps in the future. It surprised no one who knew him that, with war clouds building, Dole offered the services of his ski-wise patrol to the U.S. Army.

His initial overture was met, as he later recalled, "with polite derision," but he finally caught the ear of General George Marshall. By 1941 the Eighty-seventh Infantry Mountain Regiment was activated at Fort Lewis, Washington, and the National Ski Patrol was hired by the War Department to recruit select men for the outfit.

When it became apparent that a larger force would be required for mountain and winter warfare, the army looked to Colorado for a separate facility. Three sites were considered. Aspen, with only a remote railroad spur, was rejected, as was Wheeler, the present site of Copper Mountain, which had no railroad at all. The eventual choice was Pando, an obscure rail junction on the Eagle River midway between Leadville and Minturn. Here, Camp Hale was constructed at a cost of $28 million and the Tenth Mountain Division activated in the fall of 1942.

To say that early training went poorly would be a gross understatement. Oppressed by a miscast command that persisted in applying flatland techniques to mountain conditions and burdened by equipment that alternated between unsophisticated and unworkable, the troopers somehow persisted to achieve combat readiness. The division was either saddled with balky mules or blessed with the latest technology, a slick little oversnow vehicle called the Weasel. There was some question of which they liked best. A large sign over the entrance to the Eighty-seventh gave a broad clue: "Through these portals pass the most beautiful mules in the world."

One could write reams about the rigors and misfortunes of training. Of raw recruits from the south paralyzed by numbing cold ranging to 30 degrees below zero. Of men marched at sea-level cadence to collapse at 12,000 feet. Of an army dispatch of carrier pigeons which couldn't fly at such extreme elevation. Of makeshift artificial glaciers which melted, dooming troops to depart for Europe with no knowledge of ice climbing. A whispered slogan said it best: "Anyone who transfers from mountain training to combat is a coward."

There also could be entire books

► *The Tenth Mountain Division, 1943-44, at Camp Hale. Lt. William J. Bourke, Denver, ordering an about-face.* COURTESY, COLORADO HISTORICAL SOCIETY F-10,569, F-24,645

written about the heroics of these 12,000 men throughout the course of the Italian campaign. How they pushed relentlessly up the spine of Italy's Apennines. How, to capture a single position, Mount Belvedere, they climbed the steep escarpment of Riva Ridge under the cover of darkness to surprise the Germans in the most bitter and dramatic battle of the entire campaign. How they finally drove triumphantly out of the mountains into the Po River valley. How captured German diaries sang grudging praises of these relentless mountain troops.

Nor were the Germans alone in these plaudits. "I look upon the action of the Tenth Mountain as one of the most vital and brilliant of the Italian campaign," wrote General Mark Clark.

But it may be argued that it wasn't until after the war that the more indelible achievements of the men of the Tenth were made. Of the thousands of survivors, many returned to desk or plow. But an equal number, captivated by their new-found skills, clung doggedly to skiing, either for work or recreation. A handful made a more lasting impression as ski builders, launching the resorts and innovations in technique and equipment which catapulted the sport to its zenith.

Most prominent among them was Peter Seibert, a New Englander who first joined the Aspen Ski School, moved on to manage Loveland Basin, and then carved the massive Vail resort from the mountain which he so often had driven past on his way from Camp Hale to Denver. One of the steepest runs on what is now America's largest ski mountain has a familiar name, Riva Ridge.

Gordy Wren, who would ski jump to a fifth place in the Olympics, later became general manager at Jackson Hole, Wyoming, and Steamboat. Friedl Pfeifer,

► *Ice climbing is the perfect off-season activity for mountaineers who can't wait for the spring thaw. These frozen waterfalls east of Vail provide exhilaration and intensity for winter climbers.*
DANN COFFEY/ THE STOCK BROKER

a native Austrian once jailed as a suspicious alien at Sun Valley, distinguished himself in battle and returned to be the first manager of Aspen Mountain and later the builder of Buttermilk. Steve Knowlton, later a national champion, was the first director of the promotional organization, Colorado Ski Country. Bob Parker first became editor of *Skiing* magazine and then the marketing whiz who popularized Vail. Curt Chase became director of the Aspen Ski School. Larry Jump built that grand bastion of alpine skiing, Arapahoe Basin. Architect Fritz Benedict designed most of Snowmass and

later was a driving force behind the Tenth Mountain Trail ski-touring route, part of it near the old training ground.

Others scattered across the country—Luigi Foeger to Ski Incline, Nevada; Herbert Schneider to Mount Cranmore, New Hampshire; Kerr Sparks to Stowe, Vermont; Jack Murphy to Sugarbush, Vermont; Ed Link and Duke Watson to Crystal Mountain, Washington; Art Draper to Whiteface, New York.

There was yet another fallout from this war which gave an equally important boost to skiing. Suddenly more than 100,000 pairs of skis, boots, and poles

were available as surplus to an eager public that had heard the stories of the ski troops and wanted to try for itself. Less known is the degree to which former troopers, long-suffering under the cumbersome army gear, felt compelled to enter the outdoor equipment business. Led by innovators like Denver's Gerry Cunningham, they made dramatic improvements in every kind of gear. With skis that worked and parkas that kept them warm and new techniques which made it all seem easy, Americans began flocking to the slopes. ■

► *Nothing seen but a blur of color and speed as these racers head for the finish line.*
KAHNWEILER/JOHNSON PHOTO

► *There is another side, another season, to the Colorado high country. A quiet approach is best for fly fishing amid the summer stillness of Piney Lake, a hideaway not far from Vail.* DAVID LOKEY/VAIL-BEAVER CREEK

All the fixings

The requisites and their exquisite blend

Forget, if you dare, the snow guns. Do not be wooed by gondolas and superchairs. Lust not after slopeside restaurants and bistros. Great skiing is born, not manufactured.

In the Colorado Rockies, the mystery of conception began in the Mesozoic epoch of geologic history about 70 million years ago with a cataclysmic upthrust of subterranean strata, a great wrenching and folding which formed mountains higher than Everest. From that pinnacle everything, literally, was downhill. As much as in the raising of mountains, skiing is created by their being torn down.

It was this erosion and glaciation which determined the present form of these ski slopes—a steep pitch here for those who crave a challenge; a touch of moderation there for cruising and control; finally, a gentle slope for learning. Nowhere else in the country, perhaps in the world, do so many mountains meet all the requisites in such exquisite blend.

Then there must be snow, that most precious commodity which is not bestowed on every mountain in equal measure. It begins somewhere in a maelstrom out in the Pacific, a great clash of air currents which gathers up in a tempest of moist air and hurtles toward land, a winter storm.

The first real mountain ramparts catch most of it, but this is not true

► *Peaks like these near the Maroon Bells are key factors in weather making.*

CRAIG AURNESS/WEST LIGHT

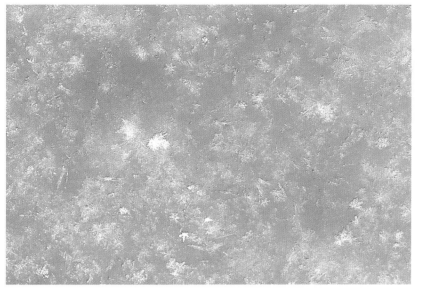

► *It all starts with a single snowflake, left. Is it true that no two are alike? Who knows. No one has seen them all.* MICHAEL S. SAMPLE

► *There is magic in snow, the way it accumulates, light and fluffy, and gleams like crystal in the sunlight, above.* MICHAEL S. SAMPLE skier's snow. Wet and heavy, it tugs at skis and nettles the soul. In the mountains of California there is a name for this snow, as heavy with derision as moisture—"Sierra cement."

The storm next passes over the deserts of the Great Basin, which soak up its excess moisture like a dry sponge before it strikes the first rampart of the Rockies, the Wasatch Range of Utah. The Wasatch claims another lion's share, but there is ample residue for Colorado. Here, higher up, it is lighter and more ethereal still. At Steamboat, which often catches the vanguard of this wintry blast, they have a more compelling name for it: champagne powder. Light, sparkling, delicate, intoxicating.

If this is a full-blown storm, it next spreads south and east, coating the broad flanks of Vail and Beaver Creek. Next comes the quadrumvirate of Summit County—Copper Mountain, Breckenridge, Keystone, Arapahoe Basin. The tempest also touches Aspen, Winter Park, Loveland, and a host of less famous ski hills.

There is one peculiarity to the snow pattern of Colorado. The resorts of the south and southwest, Crested Butte, Purgatory, Telluride, and Wolf Creek, often are fed by completely different storms circulating up over the Mexican Baja. These come less frequently but often bear more snow, saucy and spicy as their place of origin.

But there is another twist to this riddle, as tangled and convoluted as the ranges themselves.

► *Making tracks in fresh powder on the first run of the day, these skiers catch only a glimmer of the sun's warming rays.* CARL YARBROUGH/ASPEN/COLORADO SKI COUNTRY USA

The magic of mountains

A mountain is a mass of rock with its own weather. Little matter what sway the elements might hold over the rest of the landscape, the mountain is an environment to itself, a realm apart. There are times when a mountaintop thrusts out in sun-splashed splendor above a lowland fog. But almost always it is the reverse.

In a way that is both peculiar and plausible, mountains manufacture snow. The Pacific snowstorm, that great mass of moisture, might happen along only once in several days. Alone, this is not enough to accumulate the depths skiers crave, to maintain prime conditions under the relentless assault of skis and sun. In between, relief may be found in any westerly flow of moist air. As this movement comes against a mountain barrier, it is forced to rise, which causes it to cool and condense. The result is a crown of clouds, which appears constant but in reality is ever-changing. Since cool air cannot hold as much moisture, snow sprays upon the high peaks as long as the westerly flow endures.

On the other side of the crest, the opposite is true. As the wind slides downhill, it accelerates and is warmed by friction; evaporation sets in and the cloud disappears as mysteriously as it began. Under such conditions, the sky may be completely clear a few miles on either side of a mountain mass, while a ski resort tucked strategically into the lee side of the peak is showered with snow. Skiers might recall those days when only a few light flakes fall down at the base lodge, yet the upper slopes are blanketed with several inches of new powder. The stronger and moister the wind flow, the heavier the snowfall and the farther it extends from the crest of the peak.

Even in Colorado, with its near-perfect blend of snow, sunshine, and moderate temperatures, there are no guarantees with the weather. Following decades of faithful snowfall, two winters of oppressive drought, the first in the 1976-77 season, caught a disbelieving industry with its resources down. By the time the second came in the 1980-81 season, many resorts had installed some measure of artificial snowmaking capability. Now twice-bitten, all major areas have extensive networks covering hundreds of acres for manufacturing snow and providing a world of peace of mind.

This snowmaking is far more than a hedge against the ravages of drought.

Even in good snow years, man-made snow expands the season, early and late, and patches up any rough spots which may crop up in the middle. Such widespread snow insurance, coupled with the basic dependability of nature, gives Colorado an overwhelming edge in the marketplace. Vacationers can make their plans with virtual certainty that the resorts will deliver the skiing.

This hypothetical ski mountain has other geographic requisites that may escape the casual eye. It must be positioned to receive a bounty of natural snow, yet sheltered from destructive winds that might later strip it away. Also, most trails must be tilted at least ever so slightly north to avoid melting

► *Nature needs a little help sometimes. This Breckenridge snow gun adds an extra layer to the lower mountain for an earlier start to the season.* BRECKENRIDGE SKI AREA

from the winter sun.

Since Colorado has more high peaks than any other state except Alaska—54 above 14,000 feet elevation and hundreds more with crowns above timberline—there are far more potential sites from which to choose, more mountains that fit the mold. In fact, the number of Colorado ski areas is limited only by considerations of demographics, logistics, and economics. There must be enough skiers to support them, they must be reasonably accessible by air and auto, and someone with a formidable bankroll must be willing to assume the risk of development.

In recent years, the growing trend toward such popular yet expensive innovations as high-speed quadruple chair lifts has placed a demand on this bankroll that no one could have envisioned two decades ago. ∎

▶ *Few forces in nature are more powerful and awe-inspiring than an avalanche. This slide has broken from the very top of a tall peak in the San Juan Mountains of southwestern Colorado.* KEN GALLARD

When the mountains roar

They are an inevitability of the mountains, as certain as their parents, the snow and the wind. The vast majority of avalanches rumble down unnoticed into some remote ravine, the equivalent of the tree which falls noiselessly in the forest with no one to hear. But now that has changed with the recent surge in popularity of ski touring and the growing passion for back-country powder. With this new flurry of activity, more and more skiers are at risk.

Forecasters at the Colorado Avalanche Information Center in Fort Collins work overtime during periods of peril to keep skiers and travelers apprised of conditions. But there are times when the hazard is everywhere, and a person must either steer clear of the mountains or rely on his own experience and judgment. On occasion, the deadly conflict between man and snow seems almost inevitable.

In one of the earliest and most heralded avalanche incidents, the great conqueror Hannibal found himself with poor alternatives and worse judgment in his crossing of the Alps in 218 B.C. The losses were staggering: 18,000 men, 2,000 horses, and a number of elephants. In 1962, a gigantic slide, perhaps the largest in recorded history, cascaded down from the Peruvian peak Huascarán, virtually destroying a small city and killing 3,500 residents.

Not even the most seemingly civilized spot is safe. Certainly no one could have anticipated the March 1982 avalanche which descended on the popular California ski resort Alpine Meadows, crushing two buildings and a chair lift and killing seven people. In Colorado, four daredevils skiing a steep slope outside the boundaries of Breckenridge ski area were buried in February 1987, the most dramatic incident in the worst season for avalanches in the state's history. Massive slides rarely are killers at established ski resorts, principally because they are more easily anticipated and either controlled or avoided. Instead, it is the smaller perils which, unnoticed, take two skiers here, another there.

As a generic term, avalanche describes a phenomenon that might involve thousands of tons of snow cascading down with a thunderous roar for a mile or more at speeds of up to 200 miles per hour, breaking and burying everything in its path. These are among the most powerful works of nature, awesome to watch, awful to endure.

Or it may be nothing more than a quiet sloughing of snow that moves only a few yards at relatively low speed. The latter can be equally dangerous for a small ski party, for it takes no more than a foot of compacted, concrete-hard, avalanched snow to snare a person in a death grip.

For skiers who venture away from controlled and maintained trails, a bit of basic knowledge about the characteristics of snow and slopes is valuable, if not vital. The components are varied and complex, from the initial shape of the snowflake to the overall moisture content of the snow to the effect of wind in accumulating it in great catchments, ready to slide. Under the most adverse conditions, changing temperatures and texture produce a condition commonly called "depth hoar," a layer of snow crystals that have metamorphosed into the equivalent of tiny ball bearings. When a heavy coat of new snow settles on top of depth hoar on a steep slope, an avalanche is inevitable. There are numerous other factors that influence a snowslide, but for those who are not experts, one bit of knowledge is enough: Avoid any steep, exposed slope, particularly if there has been a recent and substantial snowfall.

Experienced backcountry skiers

► *A ski patrolwoman at Snowmass prepares a bomb for avalanche control.* KAHNWEILER/JOHNSON PHOTO

take other precautions. They carry electronic detection devices or trail long, colorful cords to facitlitate detection should someone be buried by snow. They space themselves when forced to cross any suspicious slope. They pay close attention to weather and snow reports.

They also pray a lot.

Superchairs:
going up in a hurry

They are called superchairs and they are to uphill ski transportation what the passenger jet is to the travel industry. With conveyor-belt efficiency, these modern marvels can whisk upwards of 3,000 skiers per hour to the top of a mountain in less time than it takes to smoke a cigarette. They delight skiers by gobbling lift lines before they even begin to form and endear themselves to management with huge savings on installation costs and operating expenses.

The notion of putting four skiers in the same chair at the same time didn't come easy. Not too long ago, designers fretted whether three might be able to mount up at the same time without creating a mayhem of tangled legs and skis in a triple chair. It wasn't until someone got the idea of taking the chair off the main drive cable and slowing it through the loading process, much like a gondola, that the quadruple chair lift arrived. My, how it has arrived.

Since Breckenridge installed the world's first detachable quad in 1981, no fewer than 17 superchairs have been added to the Colorado lift fleet, which now has more than the remainder of the nation combined.

The reason for the sudden rush is easy to comprehend. The inaugural Breckenridge quad, still the fastest in the world, transports 3,000 skiers per hour, compared with 1,800 for the best triple.

Vail's heralded Vista Bahn, which features an optional bubble-top enclosure, was installed on a track once occupied by a gondola that transported 450 skiers per hour. The Vista Bahn carries 2,650. For all their speed and efficiency, superchairs do not come cheap. Depending upon length and terrain, a quad costs about $2 million, more than twice the tab for a triple. But the superchair offers a long-term savings on maintenance and personnel.

Another marvel of the superchair is its adaptability. In areas used by expert skiers for whom rapid-fire loading is no problem or where added capacity is not yet required, they may be run on a fixed grip. But in those areas frequented by learning skiers, they may be converted to the detachable mode. This means that upon entering the loading area, the chair is temporarily derailed from the drive cable to a slower mode, allowing skiers plenty of time to seat themselves. The chair then quickly is rejoined to the drive cable, which moves at a higher rate of speed than a regular chair lift. Not only do the chairs move faster, but they may be placed closer together since timing no longer is a factor in loading.

► *Superchair atop Aspen Mountain.*
JERI WALTON

► *The Vista Bahn at Vail.*
DAVID LOKEY/VAIL-BEAVER CREEK

There also is a social advantage. Skiing companions are much more frequently found in multiples of two than of three. The triple chair often leaves an odd man out.

How popular is the superchair? When Vail installed four of them on the east side of its mountain in the 1985-86 season, the change in the traffic pattern was so pronounced that parts of the mountain seemed almost deserted. Truth is, the only trouble with the quads is that they may be too much of a magnet. Ski area managers have discovered that a companion expansion in trails and lodge facilities is required where superchairs replace conventional lifts; there is a real potential for hauling up more skiers than the traffic will bear at the expense of skiing quality.

These are relatively minor problems that are rather easily remedied, and the craze shows no sign of abating. Vail plans to build five more over the next half-decade, and others are poised to follow. Everyone seems agreed that by any gauge, this new rage in ski lifts is positively super.

► If a dog truly is man's best friend, then it deserves to go skiing, too. It's always fun and games at *Telluride.* BRUCE BENEDICT/THE STOCK BROKER

► *The cowboy tradition, exemplified here by Bill Kidd, lives and dies hard at Steamboat, where you'll find Stetsons in the lift line and on the slopes.* STEAMBOAT SKI CORP./COLORADO SKI COUNTRY USA

The best and brightest

Colorado's family of distinctive ski centers

Just as the siblings of a large family develop their individual personality traits, so, too, have Colorado's ski resorts evolved into distinctive places, each with its own diversity, its characteristic allure. That these ski centers have evolved unevenly over time and a broad range of conditions adds considerable spice to the relationships.

They are in many ways alike, these Colorado resorts, yet in even more ways different. They can be charming or challenging, demure or demanding. Seldom are they dull.

► *What better way to highlight a sunny day of skiing at Loveland Basin than with a mountain picnic.* LOVELAND BASIN SKI AREA/ COLORADO SKI COUNTRY USA

Vail, a giant on the prowl

For a time, Earl Eaton had the world's greatest ski secret. A ski patrolman at Aspen by winter, he spent summers prospecting for uranium in the mountains near his home on Squaw Creek in the Eagle River valley. It was on one of these forays that he discovered what no one else knew: the limitless potential of that long, billowing ridge which would come to be known as Vail Mountain.

For years the best skiers in the country had driven unknowingly past this nameless mountain. Ski troopers from the Tenth Mountain Division at Camp Hale and later the crowd from Aspen all passed frequently on trips back and forth to Denver. But this is a mountain that does not surrender its treasures easily. It rolls up from the valley in a series of terraces, each concealing the other, never quite revealing all that it is. Peter Seibert, a Tenth Mountain veteran and an Aspen ski instructor, didn't have to be shown twice. From that day in 1957 when Eaton brought him over to peek behind these beguiling veils, Seibert was a man obsessed.

What happened next has become the standard textbook for ski-area development, a Byzantine tale of contractual dexterity and intrigue that is repeated often in the classrooms of the nation's leading business schools. It is a tale so rich as to require no embellishment: how Seibert and his associates, taking a name from the Italian campaign, formed the Trans Montane Rod and Gun Club as a ruse to hide their real reason for purchasing the sheep ranch at the base of the mountain at a bargain price. How, in making the deal, he plied the shepherd with a strong Greek liqueur called ouzo, a name gleefully given one of the first and most popular ski runs.

That was the easy part. Next came the maddening tasks of raising money from an investment community leery of what it perceived as inordinate risks in the ski industry and of obtaining permits from a U.S. Forest Service unconvinced that Colorado's mountains needed another resort. Seibert and George Caulkins, a Denver oilman, spent months traveling across the country, relentlessly pounding

► *You'll need a couple of lessons before you try this, but cliff jumping at Vail is a tradition as old as the resort itself.*
DAVID LOKEY/VAIL-BEAVER CREEK

► *Skiing knows no bounds of age, especially if you're young of heart and body and skiing at Vail.*

DAVID LOKEY/VAIL-BEAVER CREEK

on corporate doors in an often futile attempt to sell shares in their limited partnership. By any modern gauge, the offering was laughably modest. The 100 shares sold to provide the initial capitalization cost $10,000 each, pocket change in today's market. There were few takers.

As time sped by, a major drama developed. Could Seibert and his associates get the money to begin construction before the permit expired and an incredulous Forest Service halted the entire process? Seibert sneaked in just under the wire. Against all odds, construction began in January 1962 on a resort called Vail, named after the pass just to the east on U.S. Highway 6.

There are other figures that seem equally ludicrous. The construction of four lifts, including a gondola, and the clearing of 160 acres of trails cost barely a million dollars. The gondola terminal building, which included a warming room and a small restaurant, was built for $40,000. A parking area for 650 cars and a bridge over Gore Creek cost $15,000. The entire expense of opening Vail—all lifts, trails, buildings, snow equipment, salaries, even the interest on loans—came to $1,550,000. By comparison, the 1985 construction of the Vista Bahn, a superchair which climbs the same path as the original gondola, cost $2.6 million.

The following December, amid considerable fanfare and few skiers, the ski area opened its lifts. Its growth, slow at first, then with crescendo, into the nation's premier ski resort is both a mirror and a beacon of the entire industry. Under the seat-of-the-pants direction of Bob Parker, another Tenth Mountain veteran, Vail Associates wrote the book on ski-area marketing and

► *Vail is a year-round town. Here costumed acrobats entertain spellbound onlookers at the annual Fourth of July celebration.*
DAVID LOKEY/ VAIL-BEAVER CREEK

promotion. And, from a hesitant collection of disjunctive buildings, Vail bloomed into something of a mountain metropolis that illuminates the valley for ten miles or more.

The maturation of Vail coincides almost precisely with the boom years of skiing, that period during the last half of the sixties and all of the seventies when the sport was flushed with fresh participants, massive capital expansion, and the feeling that the party would last forever.

There were reasons for the push that ran the usual gamut from sociology to economics. An unprecedented period of prosperity left many Americans eager for new horizons in recreation. Skiing, with its aura of excitement and scintillation, became all the rage. Enthusiasts

came from every direction, the cities of the Northeast, the tablelands of the Midwest and, most surprisingly, from the Sunbelt, whose denizens developed a remarkable appetite for mountain winter. Not only was skiing perceived as something of an adventure, it was something that could be shared by the entire family.

This also was the time of the great surge in air travel, when all of America went airborne. With Denver as a highly accessible hub, Vail and other burgeoning Colorado resorts were but a quick call to a travel agent away. Improved equipment, fashionable new clothing, breakthroughs in instruction—all made skiing more inviting. But it remained for that phenomenon of mountain real

estate, the condominium, to provide perhaps the most important innovation of the period. With thousands of owner-investors to share the risks, attractive and affordable lodging became available just in time to greet this horde of new arrivals. The second great gold rush was on.

Nowhere has the lode been richer than at Vail. Somewhere in the midst of this four-season hustle and bustle are 80 restaurants, bars, and nightclubs, 140 shops, 3 theaters, and lodging for 25,000 people. The reputation is international: five-star restaurants, the best merchandise, the poshest lodging. No place in all the world of skiing has more of the finest money can buy. It is not inexpensive, but no one expects it to be.

▶ *Vail's Back Bowls, larger than many other entire ski areas, draw powder enthusiasts by the tens of thousands.* DAVID LOKEY/ VAIL-BEAVER CREEK

Vail Mountain

Perhaps the most remarkable thing about Vail is that no matter how compelling the lure of the village, it never has been able to overshadow the excitement of the ski slopes. Vail Mountain is, in a word, immense. The bare numbers are impressive enough. A gondola, four superchairs, three triple chairs, nine double chairs—the largest uphill capacity in the nation. More than 3,080 acres of terrain spread over 3,150 vertical feet, including 1,903 acres of advanced-to-intermediate bowl skiing, make it the largest single ski

mountain in the nation.

Skiing here is marvelously varied, meticulously maintained, and with the 1985 addition of the superchairs, no longer crowded. The next in an endless string of developments will be the opening of China, Siberia, and Teacup bowls, a vast powder expanse on the back side of the mountain that alone is larger than most other major resorts. The pitch is slightly more gentle than that of the neighboring Back Bowls, opening this powder paradise to skiers of intermediate ability.

It is little wonder that, with so much wealth, Vail Associates decided to have a child.

Beaver Creek, the crown prince

For a resort born either four years too late or two too soon, Beaver Creek has grown into a remarkably robust youngster. No one who surveys this meticulous layout with its luxurious lodges, fashionable shops, and spectacular ski mountain—the most exclusive in all the land—ever would guess that it was an anemic child, listless, undernourished. Even in the anomalous world of skiing, its birth and early upbringing make for an outlandish tale.

Conception was conventional enough, rising from the passion of Vail Associates, the parent of Vail, for reaping the real estate windfall which had eluded it at the older resort.

Even though they clearly were the most innovative and successful ski resort developers in U.S. ski history, Vail's founders still made a colossal miscalculation. Underfinanced and having no more experience than anyone else in foreseeing such things, they bought short and wound up retaining only a small portion of the land in the long, meandering Vail Valley. While Vail Associates provided all of the impetus and assumed most of the risk, latecomers grabbed off hundreds of acres of peripheral property and reaped much of the profit.

Now all this could be made right simply by spawning a new resort. Fortuitously, there was a mountain with a private valley just ten miles to the west which would make a near-perfect cradle. This time there would be no slipup. All the land in the tight little vale formed by a picturesque stream called

► *Beautiful Spruce Saddle, high on the slopes at Beaver Creek, has few peers as a mountain restaurant and warming house.* DAVID LOKEY/ VAIL-BEAVER CREEK

Beaver Creek was purchased, and a comprehensive master plan forged to make it the most carefully designed and consummately attractive resort in the history of skiing.

There was just one problem. Even in this time of rapid growth, Colorado suddenly had a temporary glut of ski areas. Almost within a matter of months, Keystone, Copper Mountain, and Telluride popped onto the scene. In addition, there was major expansion at Breckenridge and Steamboat and immediate plans for an entire new area adjacent to Winter Park. Moreover, state officials suddenly acquired severe reservations about the pace and direction of this unprecedented mountain development. Even this prince, Vail's chosen, would have to wait.

Environmentalism was the vogue and Beaver Creek became the primary battleground. Permits were challenged, building densities reexamined. Suddenly, there was a fight over everything. With an assortment of foes storming the parapet, Vail Associates found an unlikely and equally troubled ally, the Denver Olympics.

No sooner had the Denver organizers secured the bid for the 1976 Winter Games than they began to have problems. Having wooed the International Olympic Committee with a low-cost but unworkable plan for ski sites in the snow-starved Front Range close to Denver, the organizers then began searching for more tenable alternatives. Despite its location 110 miles from the city, Beaver Creek seemed a natural: a grand ski mountain that could contain an Olympic-size downhill course, assure reliable snow, and most important, had a management eager to assume most of the expense.

It seemed the perfect symbiosis. Denver would have its sorely needed, Olympic-size alpine ski site, virtually free and clear. Vail Associates could trade on the import and immediacy of the Olympics to leapfrog all the bureaucratic hurdles for its offspring and

► *Beaver Creek, created for its alpine splendor, also has become the center of cross-country activity in the Vail Valley.* DAVID LOKEY/VAIL-BEAVER CREEK

reap the world's grandest publicity harvest in the bargain. Then the unthinkable happened. In a move without precedent, disillusioned Coloradans voted in November 1972 to withhold funding for the Olympics. The Denver Games were dead.

With no Olympic torch to follow, Beaver Creek became even more tangled in a web of red tape. By the time it finally loosened itself for the race toward its eventual 1980 opening, recession had struck, making it even more difficult to attract big-money investment. Beaver Creek's birth that sun-splashed December day was a gala affair. But there could have been a few more gifts at the baby shower. Or perhaps the party could have been postponed until the economic upturn of 1982.

Now all that is passé, no more than a wrinkle in time which even the investors who lost so much in the delay can find reason to chuckle about. There is much reason for merriment in present Beaver Creek. Owning a condominium might be one, providing it is paid for. A nice unit right by the slopes could be yours for just over a million dollars. Or you might prefer a home along the golf course for a mere $4.7 million.

Beaver Creek's magnificent ski mountain reflects the same grace and style as its splendid base development:the elegance of the Village Hall and Spruce Saddle warming houses, the posh private club right on the slopes, the rhythmic, open ski runs. When Vail plays host to the World Alpine Championships in 1989, an echo of the 1950 race in Aspen, some of the events, including the downhill, will be at Beaver Creek.

The big race may be 13 years late in coming, but well worth the wait.

At play on the slopes of the Lord

When the Reverend Don Simonton conducts his service, there is no church in the world big enough to hold it.

On many Sundays after Simonton, an ordained Lutheran minister, bids goodbye to the faithful at the Mount of the Holy Cross Church in Vail, he changes from robes to stretch pants, climbs on a chair lift, and heads up the mountain for his second message of the day. This one, bounded only by the magnificent sweep of the Gore Range, is a different kind of sermon on the mount, a communion with the outdoor world through the medium of skiing.

Simonton began Vail's "Meet the Mountain" program in 1975. It was a natural outgrowth of his abiding interest in history, ecology, and skiing and the result of a persistent request among the vacationers who came to the Sunday services he conducted at that time up on the mountain at MidVail.

"Afterward, people would come up to me and ask if I planned to ski and if I would recommend where they might go. A lot of people get lost and feel uncomfortable on a mountain this big."

The program, which has the enthusiastic support of Vail management, is designed primarily to introduce first-time visitors to the giant mountain, but Simonton adds twists certain to be of interest to everyone.

Increased demands of a growing parish do not allow him to conduct as many sessions personally as he once did, but the staff is bolstered by a number of instructors. At Beaver Creek the overseer is Simonton's son, Cliff, the environmental coordinator at that resort. The tours are Sunday, Monday, and Tuesday at Vail and Thursday and Friday at Beaver Creek. Starting time is 1 p.m., and meeting places are at Wildwood on Vail Mountain and Spruce Saddle at Beaver Creek.

"We have an interesting arrangement," Simonton explained. "The ski school pays the church rather than me directly, which helps support a small church and keeps me from being accused of moonlighting and spending too much time skiing."

It quickly becomes plain Simonton delights in his dual role, since it allows him to combine his three favorite avocations. A former director of the Colorado Ski Museum in Vail, he laces his discussions with a rich sampling of ski lore. He also is a former National Park Service employee, a background that provides him a broad knowledge of flora and fauna. Then, there is the skiing, something he enjoys unabashedly.

In a deep, rich baritone, Simonton informs a visitor of just about

► *Don Simonton in his dual role as instructor and minister on the slopes at Vail.* DAVID LOKEY

everything there is to know about Vail Mountain, from how to avoid lift lines and find the last bit of powder to the origin of the names of the trails and how the resort was founded.

All the while, Simonton keeps his group moving briskly along his favorite runs, providing a panoramic look at the massive mountain. Ski time isn't given short shrift. But there is a corresponding emphasis on the total mountain experience.

"Sniffing the flowers along the way," Simonton calls it. "There really are three kinds of recreation derived from skiing—physical, mental, and spiritual—and I don't necessarily mean spiritual in a religious sense. We shortchange ourselves when we don't go home recharged in mind and spirit rather than just tired. I've always felt there was much more to skiing than just turn, turn, turn."

There have been modifications in the schedule over the years and more adjustments are likely in the future as the resort changes and grows. But whatever the program, Don Simonton's church always has room for one more.

Aspen, queen of the Rockies

It is one of those imponderables, impossible to know but intriguing to speculate. What if this place, America's most famous ski town, had kept its original name, Ute City? Would it have come so far, flown so high, as it has under the more engaging designation, Aspen, taken from the lovely tree with the quaking leaves?

Would Jack Nicholson have bought two homes in a place called Ute City? Would Martina Navratilova have discovered the same charm? Would Ted Kennedy still come here to ski?

That an automobile and a soft drink and who knows how many other products have been given the same name is a testament to America's most successful renaming since New Amsterdam became New York. Known as Aspen since 1880, this place on a broad bench of the Roaring Fork River valley has flourished to become an international tourist mecca, more often in the news than cities a hundred times its modest population of 8,000. That these reports are not uniformly cheerful only adds to the mystique. Legends of music come here to perform, as do giants of the stage. The rich and famous flit in and out in their Lear jets, sometimes to stay for months or years, lending their cachet to both the fact and fancy of a town where image often overpowers reality. Aspen also is a town where a drug dealer is blown up by a car bomb, something which very likely never will happen in the hermetically sealed environment of Vail. It is where political wrangling is incessant, where competing newspapers often flash scandal,

► *If it's yellow, it must be a taxi. If it's mellow, it must be in Aspen.* CHARLIE MEYERS

substantial and imagined, across their front pages, where a local taxi company is called the Mellow Yellow. In short, Aspen is a true town, vibrant and vital.

This lofty tone was set just after World War II when Chicago industrialist Walter Paepcke and his wife, Elizabeth, patrons of art and architecture and athletics, shook the former silver mining camp from a half-century slumber. The Paepckes spruced up many of the old Victorian buildings, imported a succession of world-famous musicians and literary figures, and most dramatic, began the Aspen Skiing Company

(ASC). No matter how warm the year-round cultural climate, how beautiful the summer, how titillating the parade of celebrities, it is skiing that grounded Aspen to the map.

Much of the attraction comes in Aspen's diversity—four separate mountains connected by a short shuttle bus ride or an outstretched thumb. Each mirrors the variety of the town itself: the prodigious steeps of Aspen Mountain, the learner's paradise of Buttermilk, an intermediate heaven at neighboring Snowmass, and the tucked-away insouciance of Aspen Highlands.

► Left, Aspen's Winterskol, among the most flamboyant of the several winter festivals which add special flavor to the Colorado ski scene, reaches it zenith with a gala parade. The historic Hotel Jerome is in the background. DOUG LEE/TOM STACK & ASSOCIATES

► Above, the internationally famous Coors Bicycle Classic features a tour de force of the Colorado mountain highways each summer, drawing banner crowds of cycle enthusiasts and tourists alike. This sprint is through the streets of Vail. ROD WALKER/ THE STOCK BROKER

Aspen Mountain

When one first mentions Aspen skiing, thoughts go to the big mountain just above town that the early miners called Ajax. It is here that Swiss mountaineer Andre Roch surveyed the first ski trail in 1936, that the old boat tow took the first skiers uphill, that Paepcke strung his first chair lift in 1947. Aspen Mountain has been lauded for having the nation's finest expert skiing, a claim in some dispute at Jackson Hole, Sun Valley, or even Telluride. What is beyond refute is that the skiing high up there among those precipitous ridges and gulches is some of the most exciting in the world.

Bell Mountain, a separate spur marked by impeccable powder glades, is an institution in itself, a supersteep slope with its own gullies fore and aft. It is for the first delicious run down the fresh powder on the Ridge of Bell that serious skiers queue up at the bottom lifts long minutes before opening. But they might also spread out for a dash down Corkscrew or a plunge down the ominously named Elevator Shaft or any of several other trails designed to rivet the attention of even the finest skiers. For those who can handle such extreme angles, the options are nearly limitless.

Things on the big mountain never have been better. No longer are there long waits for the choice chairs—a superchair and two fixed-grip quads, all new in the last two years, have seen to

► *Aspen's Winternational, which features America's Downhill, has become one of the highlights of the World Cup calendar.* NICHOLAS DEVORE III/ PHOTOGRAPHERS ASPEN

that. But the real star in what has been an overall 33 percent gain in lift capacity is the Silver Queen gondola, a sleek, six-passenger conveyance that not only allows novice skiers—or even non-skiers—to sample the delights of the mountaintop, but carries an historic footnote as well. Just as Paepcke's initial 1947 chair lift was the world's longest, the Silver Queen can boast the planet's greatest single-stage vertical rise for a gondola, 3,250 vertical feet.

For all those skiers for whom such superlatives are a bit overwhelming, there is Buttermilk, a benign hummock of a mountain two miles outside town. If the name suggests something bland, it is true only in the immediate context; Buttermilk suffers only when compared with its more imposing neighbors. Examined separately, it is a perfectly fine mountain with a vertical drop of more than 2,000 feet and varied terrain.

That a majority of the slopes are of beginner and intermediate tilt, coupled with an insular location, make it the natural centerpiece for Aspen's vast ski school, a legion larger than the standing armies of certain Third World nations. It is here that most of Aspen's newer skiers cut their teeth, a juicy bone if there ever was one.

For many skiers, the mountains are not the dominant design in Aspen's mosaic. A grander attraction is the town itself, whose composite charms include splendid restaurants, upscale shops, lively night spots, cabaret dinner theaters,

► *The skier is world champion Steve Mahre; the race is the giant slalom at the Aspen Winternational.* DIRK GALLIAN

and a brilliantly renovated opera house as a center for a broad range of cultural events. Après-ski Aspen fairly dazzles; so lively is it that many winter visitors come here with no intent whatsoever of going near a ski lift.

Yet all is not completely well in this paradise. Oddly, Aspen's worst blemish lies very close to its beauty mark. For more than two decades, both the town and its surrounding county have operated under controversial, but widely supported, growth restrictions which have served to preserve the town's singular personality. Permits for almost any construction have been hard to come by. For major lodging properties, they have been next to impossible.

During a period in which rival resorts created luxury lodging units by the tens of thousands, Aspen's accommodations suffered comparative stagnation, growing long of tooth and short of appeal. Now, feeling a pinch in an increasingly competitive market, officials seem inclined toward compromise. The historic Hotel Jerome, first renovated by the Paepckes, has been given a splendid second facelift, with more expansion on the way. A new hotel is being molded into the lower gondola terminal by the Aspen Skiing Company, and barring further bureaucratic snares, an even larger midtown hotel seems likely under the aegis of New York real estate magnate Donald Trump. Meanwhile, most of Aspen's better lodging and nearly all of its recent growth may be found in a separate, and very different, village a dozen miles to the northwest.

▶ *Who could help but smile while skiing in Aspen powder up to the knees.* DIRK GALLIAN

The miracle workers of Aspen

Elizabeth Paepcke, still radiant near the midpoint of her ninth decade, beamed at the recollection.

"A group of us had climbed up on skins to the top of Richmond Hill, high above town, and although I was something of a beginning skier, I was amazed at what I saw.

"For miles in every direction, the snow was unbroken by so much as a rabbit track. Little veils of snow were blowing across the high peaks against the bluest sky I had ever seen. It was as if I had rediscovered the ice age, as if the world had been created all over again.

"I distinctly remember thinking what would happen when Walter got his hands on this place."

Ah, yes. Walter. Of the hundreds of thousands of skiers who stream through Aspen each year, only a handful know the name Walter Paepcke. Yet virtually everything they do and see bears the stamp of this remarkable man. The architecture, the entertainment, the skiing. Particularly the skiing.

The demands of business and war kept Paepcke away from Aspen for nearly six years after his wife's grand revelation that winter day in 1939. But once he arrived, things quickly began to happen.

To best understand what the Paepckes wrought, it is necessary to revisit the Aspen of the forties, a sleepy relic which had slipped far from its glory days as a silver boomtown. When Elizabeth first arrived, there was but one electric light in town, a naked bulb wired to the porch roof of the Hotel Jerome. Most of the quaint Victorian buildings were in acute disrepair; there was not the barest hint of the cultural center, the fairyland of the rich and famous, Aspen was to become.

Paepcke's first act was to establish the Aspen Company, whose purpose was to restore these Victorian homes and to resume operation of the historic Jerome. Stories abound about the reception he received from entrenched locals leery of the motives of this wealthy outsider, particularly when he offered to repaint their homes for free—provided he got to choose the color of the paint. It is not surprising that many refused.

Enchanted with the prospect of skiing, he sent a platoon of engineers up Ajax Mountain on a feasibility study. Encouraged by the report, he spent $250,000 to install the world's longest and fastest chair lift, and on January 10, 1947, the Aspen Skiing Company was founded.

There had been skiing on the mountain dating back to an earlier survey by Swiss avalanche expert Andre Roch. There was even an old boat tow serving a run on the lower mountain. The U.S. National Ski Championships had been held there in 1941, but now this was the big time, the sort of thing tourists would come halfway across the continent to experience.

Ever the dreamer, Paepcke next turned his attention to Aspen summer, which he envisioned as something of an American Salzburg. He proclaimed a Goethe Festival in 1949, the two-hundredth anniversary of the German philosopher, and spiced it with lectures by Albert Schweitzer and Thornton Wilder and music by Arthur Rubinstein and Gregor Piatigorsky.

He founded the Aspen Music Festival, still an annual highlight on the national classical calendar. The next project was the Aspen Institute for Humanistic Studies and Health Center to enrich the spiritual and physical health of the nation's businessmen. The institute became a model for generations of imitators and had as its motto a message perhaps even more appropriate today: Turning the executive away from the urgent to the important.

His partner in all of this was the former Elizabeth Hilken Nitze, daughter of the head of romance languages at the University of Chicago and a student at Chicago's prestigious Art Institute. She was raised in an atmosphere of intellectual accomplishment and social elegance; family friends included Prokofiev, Matisse, Rubinstein, and Piatigorsky. It was Elizabeth, then as now, who provided much of the impetus for Aspen's Renaissance.

Walter Paepcke years ago had perceived that paper boxes would replace wood for shipping and storage and quickly projected his father's simple box company into a major firm. The Chicago-based Container Corporation of America, with sales of $11.5 million in 1926, its first year, had grown to $275 million by 1960, the year Walter died.

Understanding the philosophy by which the Paepckes operated lends insight into the rejuvenation of Aspen. Convinced the corporation could sell more than boxes, Elizabeth covered them with paintings and philosophical quotations as an extension of a rare corporate credo: We believe in elegance.

Throughout, Paepcke scarcely neglected the Aspen Skiing Company, quickly attracting some of the finest talent in what still was an infant sport. From Austria, by way of Sun Valley, he lured Friedl Pfeifer, who carved many of the first trails. Dick Durrance came over from Utah to run the ski company during the 1950 World Ski Championship. Peter Seibert, the man who would build Vail a dozen years later, was an early member of the ski school.

Over the years, the legacy has grown. Aspen now is the nation's most recognizable mountain resort, winter and summer, a center of sport and culture whose fame has spread over the globe. One can only wonder if any of this would have happened if Elizabeth Paepcke hadn't chosen to make the long climb up Richmond Hill.

▶ *Snowmass is ablaze with color during an annual balloon race which attracts participants from all over the country.* GAIL DOHRMANN

Snowmass, a family affair

Snowmass might claim to be the nation's finest intermediate ski mountain, but it really doesn't need to. Almost everyone else is perfectly willing, even eager, to make the boast in its stead. A simple bill of particulars proves the case well enough. Nearly two-thirds of this immense ski mountain—1,560 acres of trails spanning 3,555 vertical feet—is composed of the kind of ego-building terrain, neither too flat nor too steep, that is prized by a majority of skiers.

Within this composite, certain parts stand out. The Big Burn, a broad expanse of timberline terrain that gets its name from a fire set more than a century ago by Ute Indians to discourage white settlers, leaving little but gnarled and bleached shells in its wake, may be the single finest patch of intermediate ski terrain in creation. There are few grander exhilarations in all of skiing than cruising through this ghost forest on a carpet of fresh snow. Better still, it is within the grasp of skiers of all abilities.

At the eastern rim of the complex is Elk Camp, more than 3,000 vertical feet of straight-shot skiing with a run 3.7 miles long. In between is the even more spacious High Alpine, which includes a magnificent concession to experts, the twin plunges of Hanging Valley Wall and Hanging Valley Glade, and farther west, the ominous Rock Island, which

▶ *The largest working sled-dog kennel in the nation is one of the attractions at Snowmass's Krabloonik Restaurant, where the unusual also extends to the plate.* SNOWMASS RESORT ASSOCIATION

► *This Snowmass cliff jumper has reached the moment of truth, but minus a ski. Does he know? Does he care?* DIRK GALLIAN

is not named for a city in Illinois. A few moguls also are allowed to grow on the runs served by the Campground lift, but there is little else about Snowmass that is not perfectly suited to laid-back cruising.

It is this abundance of broad middle ground that sets the tone for Snowmass's reputation as a place for families. All members, no matter what age or ability, can ski here with comfort and as much community as they choose. Then there is the matter of convenience. More than 90 percent of the lodges, most of them attractive and of recent vintage, are accessible from the ski trails, a further boon to family ease. All of this funnels into a compact pedestrian mall, also within reach of every ski or shoe. On the slopes or in the village, the urge to roam is never stifled; even the littlest ramblers can follow their wanderlust without trepidation.

There are diversions enough: sleigh rides, ice skating, repertory theater, an exceptionally fine ski touring center, and that most uncommon of all dining experiences, a jaunt through the woods by dog sled to the Krabloonik Restaurant, also the site of the world's largest working kennel for huskies.

Another attraction stands out. Every morning the weather allows, the Snowmass sky is filled with the brightly colored spheres of hot-air balloons, which take visitors aloft to view the soaring vistas down the valley and generally have them back in the village for most of a morning of skiing.

Little wonder that more than half the skiers who come to Aspen make Snowmass their base.

At night, Snowmass is somewhat subdued, a quiet hideaway of comfortable yet unpretentious restaurants removed from the hurly-burly of Aspen, yet close enough for visitors to nip over for a taste of excitement when the urge strikes. For those who choose, wicked old Aspen is but a short drive or a quick bus away.

But there is a newer, more lively Snowmass waiting in the wings. Just as the Hanging Valley addition lent double-black-diamond stimulation to the mountain, so, too, will Phase Three of the mall development bring expansion and renovation to a village that already has skiing's finest conference center. Shops will be expanded, restaurants upgraded, and bright new additions made to an existing bed base for more than 8,000 guests.

There'll be something else as well. At the center of all this new liveliness will be Snowmass's first disco. Lock up the children. Clear the streets. Is no place safe anymore?

Aspen Highlands, a well-kept secret

It isn't easy to hide a ski area with a vertical descent of 3,800 feet, one whose summit rises 11,800 feet into the clouds. The task becomes even more difficult when this behemoth is situated just a couple of miles from one of the world's most famous ski towns. Aspen Highlands does its best.

Highlands hasn't actually tried to remain invisible, but in nearly three decades of existence, things have sort of worked out that way. The problem has nothing at all to do with the viability of Highlands as a ski place. It is a perfectly fine mountain with a wide variety of terrain, unbelievably long and rambling intermediate and beginner runs punctuated by expert chutes which dive off either side of the broad main ridge, and for good measure, perhaps the most breathtaking single view in all of American skiing. From the high-wire suspension of the Loges chair lift near the top of the mountain, it seems as if one can almost reach out and touch the soaring twin turrets of the Maroon Bells.

Instead, the reason for this relative obscurity is that Highlands, tucked away in its own private valley out of the mainstream, is overpowered by Aspen's three other mountains, all owned by the giant Aspen Skiing Company, North America's most prolific operator of ski lifts. For all these years, it has played Oakland to the ASC's San Francisco, Harpo to Groucho. It would be accurate enough to pass this off as a simple case of a large enterprise outshining a small one, but this would give short shrift to Highlands' unique personality and the ongoing intrigue between these mismatched rivals. Surprisingly, the big guy hasn't always come out on top.

To fully understand the true nature of Highlands, one first must know the charming eccentric who founded it. As unlikely as his name, Whipple Van Ness Jones began the ski area on a relative shoestring, yet he remains the only founder still in control of a major Colorado resort and one of a tiny handful of individual owners. Jones is a standout among the business herd, one who not only dares to be different, but insists on it.

"I guess I've always been something of a nonconformist," Jones once said. "I suppose it's because with a name like Whipple Van Ness Jones, I had to fight my way to school every day. Things sort of progressed from there."

While the rest of Aspen swept off into the jet stream, Highlands moved at its own pace, unhurried, laid back. With its separate teaching method, pricing schedule, and promotions, it evolved as something of a skiing counterculture with a band of local loyalists similarly devoted to twisting the tail of the corporate giant just across the valley.

Over the early part of its life, Highlands primarily was a hangout for Aspen residents drawn by the lure of camaraderie, an inexpensive season pass, and the rock-firm assurance that they wouldn't be troubled much by the kind of people who came to town in a Lear jet. Then the inevitable happened. The tourists, no dullards, started to wonder what it was about the place the locals liked so much. It would be gross exaggeration to suggest that Highlands has become overrun with skiers, that stretch suits with fur collars have taken over the slopes, that funk has given way to fancy.

But things at least partially have changed, mostly in reflection of the times, the rest a result of a celebrated lawsuit in which Jones and his slingshot at least temporarily stopped the giant in its tracks. Charging the Aspen Skiing Company with an antitrust violation in refusing to cooperate in the sale of a four-area lift ticket, Highlands won a $7.5 million judgment and a world of publicity. There now is an interchangeable ticket, but the rivalry has not subsided.

More recently, Highlands has pushed to alter its iconoclastic image. There is a plan afoot, thus far rejected by a

▶ *Aspen Highlands' 3,800-foot vertical drop is the greatest in the state. That's 14,018-foot Pyramid Peak in the background.*
ASPEN HIGHLANDS/ COLORADO SKI COUNTRY USA

growth-conscious county government, to build a hotel and shopping village. A companion project that would upgrade the lifts and add new trails has been placed in abeyance until the base development is approved.

All this delay may be for the best. If they did all that fancy construction, tourists might actually discover the place.

► *Steamboat, which has blossomed from a sleepy ranch community to become one of the nation's premier resorts, still glistens after the lifts close.*

STEAMBOAT SKI CORP./ COLORADO SKI COUNTRY USA

Steamboat Springs, Ski Town, U.S.A.

It is a night in late February, crisp and bright under a full moon. The highway route from the east through the snow tunnels on Rabbit Ears Pass resembles nothing so much as a wide-set bobsled run, a portent of the powder waiting at the ski resort just minutes ahead.

The road plunges down, down, a rambling corkscrew of disorientation on a blank tapestry of white. One final turn and this sameness opens up into a twinkling ocean of lights, for all the world like the glow of a miniature Las Vegas, shimmering with excitement and intrigue. Could this really be Steamboat Springs, the sleepy little cow town where the old Norwegian, Carl Howelsen, made his most notable landfall in the teen years of this century? Where a rancher-engineer named John Fetcher hauled the first little chair lift up from Denver in 1962 on a flatbed truck? Where generations of Olympians, more than from any other ski town in the country, sprang from Howelsen Hill, the tiny hummock above town named for the Norseman?

This, after all, is Steamboat, not Vail or Aspen or any other of those glitzy, sparkle-and-shine resorts where people prance around in diamonds and furs. Forget the dazzling lights for a moment. When dawn comes, Steamboat still is a place where leather is used for saddles and vests and boots, never trousers.

Steamboat remains a town where tradition runs deeper than the snow they call, with pardonable ostentation, champagne powder. The lineage is direct and long, beginning in February

► *Ghost trees, created when heavy snow sticks to evergreeens like multiple layers of spray paint, are a common occurrence on Steamboat's Storm Peak.* LARRY PIERCE

▶ *The Steamboat Winter Carnival, oldest in the state, features street races such as skijoring, a combination of a cow-town past and a skiing future. Another carnival highlight is world-class ski jumping.*
KEVIN SAEHLENOU/STEAMBOAT SKI CORP./
COLORADO SKI COUNTRY USA

1914 when Howelsen helped organize a winter carnival that now has been repeated without interruption, the most enduring such event in the nation.

Confident of his love affair with this strange amalgam of cowboys and skiing, Howelsen bought a small house in Strawberry Park, an enclave two miles outside of town. From this vantage point, he quickly convinced the citizenry of the need for a jumping hill, choosing a steep slope on the hillside just above the Yampa River, a hill that later would bear his name.

In 1916 a Norwegian named Ragnar Omtvedt of Howelsen's old Chicago club broke the world ski jump record by more than 15 feet, soaring 192 feet and 9 inches, on the hill that Carl had prepared. Anders Haugen, a naturalized American who later would win the only U.S. Olympic ski jumping medal, a bronze, finished second that day. To the total delight of a screaming crowd of townsfolk, local boy Henry Hall broke Omtvedt's record with a jump of 203 feet the very next year.

Thus a lineage of Steamboat ski heroes was begun, a line of succession that has remained unbroken. No one understands it better than John Steele.

"I was a boy of 12 or so and my house was located on Howelsen's route to the ski hill," recalls Steele. "I kept a lookout and always was ready to go when he came by. All those days watching him, listening to what he taught me, made me everything I was."

What John Steele became was Steamboat's first Olympian, a competitor in the 1932 games at Lake Placid, and the role model for dozens who would follow.

One story stands out among the rest. Fresh from competing as a ski jumper in the Winter Olympics, Steele steps onto the stage of the tiny school auditorium. Resplendent in his team warm-up, he speaks of his pride in competing for his country and tells enchanting tales of great skiers from other lands. In the back of the room, a boy, small for his age, leaps to his feet and shouts loud enough for all around to hear.

"I'm going to do that," says young Gordy Wren. "I'm going to ski in the Olympics." Sixteen years and a world war later, Wren did just that, the only American skier ever to qualify in four events. As they all have, sooner or later, Wren returned to Steamboat to coach the three Werners—Skeeter, Buddy, and Loris—and Marvin Crawford and Katy Rodolph and Moose Barrows and the two Elliots, Jere and Jon. Olympians all, trained on old Howelsen Hill, so small that a single surface lift easily runs all the way to the top.

This was the climate in which the ski resort was launched from the bed of Fetcher's ranch truck on a big mountain just southeast of town, the one that was renamed Mount Werner after Buddy was killed in an avalanche in 1964. The news that the Steamboat ski area had opened did not make the business pages or even the sports section. The entire operation revolved around a lonely A-frame that today wouldn't make a suitable ticket office. The single lift spanned a distance barely long enough for a good-sized slalom course.

Somehow, against all reckoning, the place kept growing: a lift here, two more there, often spreading up and out by leaps and bounds. Now, at one of its rare resting points, Steamboat spans 1,400 groomed acres, 18 chair lifts, and a new state-of-the-art gondola, the Silver Bullet, which whisks 2,800 passengers per hour (in 128 eight-passenger cabins) 2,200 vertical feet up to the top of Thunderhead. Depending upon the standard of measurement, Steamboat ranks either as the third- or fourth-largest ski resort in the nation, after Vail, Mammoth, and Killington. Mark it up to the magnetism of the mountain, an irregular mass whose varied crests, one upon another, conceal a succession of secrets that have kept skiers—and developers—coming back for more. Or it could be the snow, often among Colorado's first flakes, enough to transform

► *Skiing is a family affair at Steamboat Springs, and this family is having a ball.*
STEAMBOAT SKI CORP./
COLORADO SKI COUNTRY USA

the ski runs into a winter wonderland.

Every resort has a specialty, large or small. At Steamboat, it is trees. By nearly any gauge, the tree skiing high up near the crest is the best in the country, if not the world. Runs like Shadows and Twilight, thatched with an amalgam of spruce and aspen, form the ultimate in timber bashing. Steep terrain, deep snow, and thick-set trees place a keen demand upon ability. A false turn may exact a heavy price, a limb for a limb.

There is more of the same at a place called Big Meadow on the north side of the complex, and up near the summit at a crown called Storm Peak, one finds the most distinctive of all Steamboat attractions, ghost trees. By some meteorological quirk, storms which strike the mountaintop a certain way plaster the spruce with snow as thick as cake frosting. There it stays for days or

weeks, piled in solid layers. Is there really a tree under all that?

Despite the magic of the trees and a scattering of straight-shot mogul chutes, Steamboat basically is a rambling teddy bear of an intermediate mountain second only to Snowmass for ears-back cruising. Long, broad runs like High Noon and Vagabond are the ultimate in carefree wandering.

While the ski mountain has doubled and tripled and the condominiums and lodges at the base have spread like spores, there is another element of Steamboat which remains essentially unchanged. In its early years, the resort was run almost exclusively by home-grown locals for whom open friendliness was not a corporate mandate, but a way of life. Even now that the work force has become more diverse, you'll still find lots of grins and howdies at Steamboat. That's just the way it is.

The Werners: Colorado's first family of skiing

The big house, its massive logs even darker in the shade of the spreading pine tree, seems little changed from that day in 1943 when Ed and Hazel—better known as Pop and Hazie—Werner bought it, moving their three young children off the ranch and into town for good. Skiing in America hasn't been the same since.

To the Werners, a house in town had far greater meaning than merely escaping the rigors of ranch life. A place in Steamboat Springs meant that the Werner children would be able to ski every day with few distractions. There were three of them. Gladys, known as "Skeeter" since infancy for her penchant for flapping her arms and legs, and Buddy, two years her junior, already were promising young skiers. Loris, still a babe-in-arms, was far from any thought of his role in skiing history.

Now the record concerning this marriage of family and mountain is complete. Until the twins Phil and Steve Mahre came to prominence in 1979, Buddy Werner, who suffered an untimely death in 1964 in a Swiss avalanche, was hailed as the finest American male skier of all time, qualifying for three Olympics and three World Championships. Skeeter made the Olympics in 1952 and two World Championships. Loris, also an outstanding ski jumper, was a member of the U.S. team for nine years and skied in the 1968 Olympics.

For the Werner family, skiing was a natural foil for winter's boredom, reflecting Steamboat's long tradition in the sport and Pop's own keen interest. Self-taught, he often took his barrel staves up into the deep snow on Rabbit Ears Pass and soon had the kids following behind him, playful as bear cubs.

Although times were tough, the Werners managed to make things fun. A racing weekend always began with Hazie's hamburgers in a brown paper bag, enough to last for days. Skeeter recalls a particularly festive occasion at the old lodge at timberline on Berthoud Pass, where Pop built a fire from wood he brought in the car.

"Hazie put on a pot of chili and we wound up feeding half the area. Whatever anyone had was shared back then. Nobody had much."

Al Wegeman, another of those early Steamboat ski greats, began the first organized ski program on Howelsen Hill about the time Skeeter hit junior high. Then Gordy Wren came back from the 1948 Olympics and the pace accelerated.

"Gordy was way ahead of the other coaches of that time. He demanded your best and if you couldn't ski for him, you couldn't for anyone," Skeeter remembered. "He was tough, just like a good father. He'd chew you out one minute and love you to death the next. We couldn't bear to let him down."

Wren's pied-piper spell brought young skiers from all directions. One year the program had 69 beginners in a community where horses outnumbered people. When it came time for the 1950 Junior Nationals, five from Steamboat qualified, and Wren loaded them all in a car and drove straight through to Stowe, Vermont, stopping just once for a meal at a roadside inn. Skeeter won the downhill and slalom, Marvin Crawford ruled the men for the second straight year, and little Buddy, just 13, gained the experience he needed to dominate the competition for years to come.

Sometimes it is hard to know whether the Werners are so much entwined with Steamboat or if it's the other way around. When the ski resort was begun in 1961, two miles east of town on a big mountain called Storm Peak and later renamed Mount Werner, Skeeter and Buddy were there with the first ski shop, now expanded to one of the state's finest. Loris now is vice-president in charge of mountain operations at Steamboat Resort.

After a new gondola was installed it didn't take long to think of a name for the plush restaurant at the summit. You won't find hamburgers and chili on the menu at Hazie's, perhaps because the fancy chef knows he couldn't match the originals.

Steve Bradley and his magnificent snow machine

It perhaps was inevitable that someone invent a snow grooming machine, a device for reducing nettlesome moguls and crud to a consistency more pleasing to skiers. But until Steve Bradley, a former Dartmouth College racer and prospective art professor, wandered west to Colorado, no one did.

In the early days of the sport, skiers had no assurance of the conditions they might encounter when they arrived on the slopes. If it snowed, there might be delightful powder. Often, the snow turned to crust or hard pack. Always there were moguls, those knee-jarring bumps that grow taller wherever skiers congregate. In the main, skiing was not a sport for the faint of heart; learning to ski under such uncertain conditions required courage and a lot of determination.

Eager to boost attendance, mountain managers realized that something must be done to make at least some of the slopes smoother to attract beginners, but options were limited. Skiers were induced with the promise of a free lift ticket to foot pack certain runs, and luckless employees were dispatched with shovels to wage a losing war against the moguls. For skiers, particularly less skilled ones, the result was not something likely to encourage many repeat visits.

A military film maker during the war, Bradley had come to Aspen as an official at the 1950 World Ski Championship. Staying on, he soon was offered the job of managing Winter Park, a ski area owned by the city of Denver that was becoming increasingly popular with skiers along the Front Range. Perhaps drawing upon a natural eye for design, Bradley envisioned a contraption that, powered by gravity, simultaneously would flatten the moguls and pack the snow.

With the help of Ed Taylor, a snow physicist, Bradley's ideas began to take shape. For the 1956-57 season, he produced a device which had a wooden roller with slats and a blade. Although gravity would cause it to roll downhill, it required a skier to serve as a steering mechanism. The task fell to a hapless ski patrolman who had the unenviable task of wrestling the 700-pound packer-grader while somehow keeping his speed controlled through mountainous moguls with a leg-burning snowplow. There were few volunteers.

Jerry Groswold, Winter Park's current president and a mountain employee during Bradley's early days, remembers that patrolmen got "flight pay" for running the device.

"They were paid ten cents an hour above scale, which now seems absolutely ridiculous. It was a terrifying piece of equipment and how we never killed anyone is beyond me.

"There was a safety device of sorts which involved a springloaded crank on the blade. If something went wrong, the operator was supposed to turn away from the tongue, which released the crank and drove the blade into the snow, stopping the whole thing dead. It's a miracle that no one got run over."

Groswold recalls another remarkable aspect about this revolutionary device, which remains on display at the Colorado Ski Museum in Vail.

"The intriguing thing to me is that the basic principle is the same one we still use today on our fancy, high-powered snowcats. The only difference is we get up and down the hill a lot faster."

Bradley's packer-grader also had a virtue that extended far beyond its ability to chop down moguls. It could compact and smooth fresh snow to provide the kind of unbroken surface learning skiers require for comfort and consistency. When word got out about the area's superior snow conditions, skiers came running from miles around.

Bradley's packers originally were carried back uphill hooked to a surface lift, but the advent of more powerful motorized snow machines in the sixties produced a system by

► *When darkness falls, it is time for the night cats to prowl, grooming the slopes for another day of skiing.* ROD WALKER/WINTER PARK

which the roller could be dragged everywhere by a machine. Given this advantage, blades and rollers became more sophisticated and the modern era of snow grooming bloomed to full flower. Along with streamlined travel and vastly improved equipment, no other development has done so much to facilitate the rapid growth of the sport.

Today, skiers may choose among trails which run the gamut of conditions, from powder to moguls. But those who love their slopes ballroom smooth should say a little prayer of thanks to Steve Bradley and his amazing packing machine.

Winter Park, the light at the end of the tunnel

There is more to the boast than meets the ear. When Winter Park calls itself Colorado's favorite ski resort, the suggestion extends far beyond the claim that more residents of the state ski here than at any other resort. The inference, there for all to hear, is that this is the place of choice for skiers who have the best of everything at their fingertips.

To find out why this is true, one must peel back several layers of the richest ski history and perhaps even delve into the psychology of paternalism. Winter Park, old and enduring, is, if not Colorado's own, certainly Denver's. The very name tells part of the story. When a visionary named George Cranmer, then manager of the Denver Department of Parks and Improvements, got the notion in 1940 for a mountain playground where city dwellers might escape the tedium of the colder months, he called it, simply, Winter Park.

From an initial investment of just $200,000 and an additional seeding of $75,000, this unique civic enterprise has grown into a complex that soon may be the second largest in the nation after Vail and, not least, a public utility valued in the tens of millions. If pride in ownership is one of the hallmarks of affection, then the brag may be beyond challenge.

It scarcely is surprising that Cranmer chose this site, just 67 miles northwest of Denver where U.S. 40 meets the floor of the Fraser River valley after its winding journey over Berthoud Pass.

► *Winter Park's new ski center for kids, perhaps the largest and most progressive in the world, reflects the resort's longstanding family appeal.* JOHN KENNEDY/WINTER PARK

Thirteen years earlier, in 1927, the equally imaginative David Halliday Moffat had punched a six-mile-long tunnel through the Continental Divide to give the nation a long-awaited central rail route through the Rockies. Not long after, a pioneer band of Denver skiers formed the Colorado Arlberg Club and cut their own ski run where the tunnel's west portal peeked out of the rock. Cranmer nestled his fledgling endeavor right in between the Arlberg Club and the tracks. Before long, the ski trains started to roll in, the beginning of a long

and enduring marriage between Winter Park and the train that has been consummated in railroad names for buildings, lifts, and trails. With a weekend ski train for transport and a short drive as an alternative, little wonder that residents of a rapidly growing Denver metroplex embraced a romance that has lasted for decades.

A few fickle suitors began to drift away to the siren song of Vail and later to the seductive variety of Summit County. Then, just when it seemed as if the romance might fade, the old girl put on a new look called Mary Jane, complete with a fetching bonnet of expert terrain with a thicker layer of powder and enough bumps and grinds to draw whistles from even the most aloof skier.

Even the name is loaded with mischief. Legend has it that Mary Jane was a sporting woman of such favor among local prospectors that the district's most promising mine was named for her. When the new Mary Jane expansion, with its equally alluring runs, was completed near the old mine site in 1975, it seemed a natural. Now Winter Park is on the move again with a second enticing growth spurt that, when completed in the mid-1990s, will represent an expenditure of $60 million covering a vast expanse of terrain that will make this the second-largest ski complex on the continent behind Vail.

Part of it already is done, including an inveigling swatch of powder glade skiing called, for reasons of history and titillation, Mary Jane's Backside. This terrain over the crest initially was opened in 1986 without benefit of a lift; skiers merely plunge over the back, dance through the glades, and then follow a gravity contour around the ridge to the lifts on the front. When the package is complete, there will be four lifts in this area, one to the top of an immense timberline bowl called Parsenn. From the pinnacle, a powder hound can plunge through 1,250 vertical feet of open snowfields which, because they provide so much room to wander, can be explored by anyone of solid intermediate ability.

Another, even larger, expansion has begun, appropriately, beyond the Looking Glass. That name was given an earlier addition of enchanting beginner-intermediate slopes with an Alice-in-Wonderland theme and storybook trails like White Rabbit, Mad Hatter, and March

Hare. The great sweep of terrain to the west is called Vasquez for the creek and mountain at the stream's source. More precisely Vasquez represents a series of ridges and valleys that someday may hold

a separate base village and ten more lifts, bringing the number to 36, enough to transport 43,700 skiers per hour and accommodate 23,500 per day. Vasquez's initial phase, served by the Pioneer Express

► *There is no such thing as starting them too young at Winter Park.*
BRUCE BENEDICT/THE STOCK BROKER

superchair, already is in place.

There are other, grander plans afoot. A private developer conditionally has agreed to string a gondola, later to be turned over to the resort, from his condominium complex near the town of Winter Park to a high point on the shoulder of the ski mountain, providing novel, off-site access to the trails. Such largess is consistent with the rapid evolution of base development. Once lacking in amenities, the resort now has a thriving village with good restaurants and attractive shops. Lodging, too, has come alive; the many condominium complexes that span the four miles between the mountain and the neighboring town of Fraser are some of the plushest accommodations in all of skiing.

All this does not mean that Winter Park has turned from the basics which made its early reputation as a no-nonsense place to ski. You'll still find more jeans than Bogners on these slopes. There's also something else here, a sense of service and responsibility consistent with the resort's civic origins. It is no surprise that Winter Park boasts the world's largest skiing program for the disabled or the finest children's center. Little wonder that the allegiance has remained so strong.

Daring to try

Deep in the bowels of West Portal Station at the base of Winter Park ski area, a group of skiers chatters noisily amid a clutter of boots, skis, and other accoutrements of a sport that runs on its equipment.

It takes but a moment's glance to know this is no gaggle of tourists in for a vacation, no ordinary ski crowd. Some have only one leg, or no legs at all. Others try to support themselves on limbs that splay out in every direction like rag dolls. There are people whose physical and mental reactions have been dulled by birth defects; a few stare blankly through eyes which cannot see.

But instead of depression, there is outlandish laughing and joking, the usual residue of an exhilarating day on the slopes. Apart from the obvious physical differences, they could be mistaken for any band of skiers alive with après-ski excitement. Back in an adjacent office, a darkly handsome man surveys the happy throng from behind a cluttered desk and breaks into a broad smile.

Hal O'Leary has viewed this tableau often and never tires of it. In the 17 years he has directed the Winter Park Handicap Recreation Program, O'Leary has helped more than 5,000 persons immerse their physical problems in the healing flow of skiing. The largest organization of its kind in the world, it employs 22 staff members and is further supported by up to 900 volunteers. In the last three years alone, the program has dispensed an average of 14,000 lessons involving 2,500 persons each season.

The quality of instruction is outstanding; Winter Park's disabled racers are the best in the world, winning championships wherever they go. But the most enduring product is an unbroken chain of individual successes that don't show up in something so dramatic as a race result. These are people who have discovered physical and emotional fulfillment through the medium of winter recreation.

The concept is as effective as it is basic. Through the activity of skiing, disabled persons gain a feeling of motion and achievement that translates to a sense of invigoration and improved self-worth. Many of these triumphs have been well chronicled. Much has been written of the people who arrived on crutches and soon became champions, of the skiers with one leg who now ski better than most with two.

But the story of how O'Leary put it all together is equally compelling —and almost as unlikely.

Born in Montreal, he spent much of his early life carting a business degree somewhat aimlessly among jobs he describes as uniformly boring. It was while working for the U.S. Army Corps of Engineers at a military base in Labrador that he came to a sudden, if somewhat novel, realization.

"I found I really enjoyed being with Americans and I decided right

► *Whether racing or bashing through expert terrain, Winter Park's handicapped skiers have demonstrated their ability to ski with anyone. This landmark program has become a standard for providing recreational opportunities for the disabled.*
KRISTIN RUD/WINTER PARK

then to emigrate."

A skier since the age of five, he gravitated towards the slopes of Colorado.

But he still was drifting at loose ends in Denver when he learned of a job managing a motel in Winter Park. The next step was to become a ski instructor and, from that, another of those momentous decisions that helped shape his and thousands of other lives.

Children's Hospital of Denver planned a ski trip as a part of its rehabilitation program, and when the ski school supervisor asked for volunteers, O'Leary's was the only hand that went up.

"I was looking for something to renew my interest in skiing," explained O'Leary, a sturdy, athletic man of 49 who could pass for ten

years younger. "At that point, I was thinking of quitting because I had become bored teaching the same old ordinary people."

The first thing O'Leary did was fashion a crude pair of outriggers and try to ski three-track with one ski, just like someone with only one leg. There were no guidelines, and as he went along, O'Leary found himself literally writing the book on teaching disabled persons to ski. Since then, people have come from all over the world to learn from him. Through an almost-perfect symbiosis, Winter Park has become a model program for rehabilitation efforts everywhere, and O'Leary has become a man reborn.

"These people have been such an inspiration to me," O'Leary said. "Sometimes it's difficult to

determine which of us gets the most from it all."

Utilizing O'Leary's formulas and devices, participants make marvelous strides in achieving a sense of worth and independence through skiing.

"People who normally have very little mobility or rhythm can realize a fluidity of motion, a freedom of movement for the first time in their lives," O'Leary explained. "Skiing is a tremendous release for those who previously were never allowed to explore their outer limits, to feel a rush of excitement. For many, skiing becomes a rapid road to at least partial physical recovery."

O'Leary makes a practice of skiing with the same simulated disabilities and equipment to fully comprehend the students' problems, even blindfolding himself to emulate the

more than 100 blind skiers in the program.

"Even after all these years, I never cease to be amazed at the courage these people muster to do the things they do," he marveled.

At Winter Park, there are thousands of disabled skiers who are forever grateful that Hal O'Leary showed his own kind of courage when he raised his hand that day.

Ski the Summit

► *Wide-open bowls above timberline make Breckenridge a favorite of powder skiers.*

BRUCE BENEDICT/BRECKENRIDGE SKI AREA

There was a time in the early evolution of that sometimes-cooperative, always-competitive confederation called Ski the Summit when the unofficial skier's guidebook contained an unflagging mandate. The unwritten command was to socialize in Breckenridge, take lodging at Keystone, explore at Arapahoe Basin, and ski Copper Mountain. With the unprecedented development that transformed these Summit County resorts, each no more than 15 miles apart, into the nation's largest interconnected ski center, these old delineations have melted away. All have grown into well-rounded resorts with all bases covered.

The Kingdom of Breckenridge

It seems only right that the one American ski resort to span three separate mountains also would at some point in its long history have its own navy, boast a separate national political autonomy, and find an occasion to tweak a vice president.

Breckenridge pitches itself as "Genuine Colorado," which, when one considers that it is 128 years old and the most ancient of ski towns, seems a reasonable claim. There is history here,

dripping from every tin roof with the melting snow. This was one of the mining camps that Father John Dyer, the itinerant minister-mailman, visited on his snowshoe circuit, delivering parcels and prayer in equal parts. It is where the Barnum & Bailey Circus once performed for eager sourdoughs, but only after the elephants had been unloaded to help push the faltering train over Borcas Pass.

It should be no surprise that such a perpetrator of illusion as P.T. Barnum should come to a place which was founded on a clever ruse. It seems that General George Spencer, leader of a faction bidding to gain control of the

► *Ancient and stylistic, telemark skiing has found a new home in Summit County and a regular spot on the Breckenridge racing calendar.* CARL SCOFIELD/ BRECKENRIDGE SKI AREA

fledgling gold camp, decided to name it after Vice President John Cabell Breckinridge on the presumption that such patronization might yield a coveted post office. But when the Civil War broke out and the politician hopped to the Confederate side, enraged residents changed the first "i" to "e" in protest.

Less than a decade later, Breckenridge's penchant for scam was back in the fore. This time it was Sam Adams, an adventurer of sorts, who got the notion of claiming a longstanding bounty offered by the government for the discovery of a northwest passage. Adams figured that the Blue River, which flowed through town and then down to the Colorado River, was the first leg of his journey to riches. He convinced idle miners and moneyed backers to build four boats and furnish the necessary supplies, and in 1869, he gathered up his flotilla and set sail. Just 60 miles downstream, shortly after joining the Colorado near the present town of Kremmling, the Breckenridge Navy was splintered on the impassable rapids of Gore Canyon.

Perhaps the reason Breckenridge today is so favored by skiers from Texas is a shared bond of independence with the Lone Star state. By some cartographer's error, the territory surrounding the town was not properly annexed as a part of the Louisiana Purchase, an oversight that has allowed the self-styled Kingdom of Breckenridge an excuse for a No Man's Land celebration each year.

There are other reasons for jubilation in Breckenridge these days. Gold brought only temporary fortune, but there has been lasting, and growing,

► *Ice sculptures abound, right, during Ullr Fest, the Breckenridge carnival dedicated to the Norwegian god of skiing.*
JEFF UHRLAUB/THE STOCK BROKER

► *Far right, wild runs and even broader vistas are staples of the Breckenridge experience.*
RICK GODIN/BRECKENRIDGE SKI AREA

prosperity with skiing. From a hesitant beginning in 1961, Breckenridge has blossomed as the second-most-popular ski resort in the state with more than 900,000 skier visits per season. Such expansion, by leaps and bounds over the last decade, has come with the takeover of the mountain operation by the giant Aspen Skiing Company in 1970 and a companion resurgence of the little Victorian town.

What once was one ski mountain now is three. Early miners, more inclined toward pragmatism than poetry, gave the majestic peaks of the Tenmile Range numerical designations. Thus the first ski development was Peak Eight, an equally unimaginative piece of territory that earned the area the derisive tag of "Breckenflats."

With the opening of the adjacent Peak Nine, the development of the saucy terrain between the two, and the unveiling of the expert glades of the Back Bowls, the resort's overall tilt became more pronounced. Then in 1985 the company strung a superchair up into the challenging powder glades of Peak Ten, and the image of too much easy skiing became just another ghost of Breckenridge's past. This is a ski complex that has made so many changes in such a short time that it created something of a reality gap. What many skiers thought was still a big, cuddly teddy bear of a mountain really had turned into a ripsnorting grizzly.

The extent to which misconception has reigned is illustrated by the hoopla surrounding a precipitous, moguled run called Mach I, which many believed to be Colorado's steepest. Truth is, it isn't even tops at Breckenridge, an honor that goes instead to a run called Tom's Baby, named after a 13-pound gold nugget found in a local mine. The Baby is but one of several chutes that nose-dive into a gully off a flank of Peak Nine. The names set the stage well enough: Mine Shaft, Devil's Crotch, Hades, Satan's Inferno.

Perhaps nothing points the direction of the new Breckenridge better than the Colorado Superchair on Peak Eight, a 2,800-passenger-per-hour detachable quad—the resort's third—which scales all of Peak Eight in a single bound, trimming the ride to the top by more than half and erasing any lift-line jam at the base. With the lift change came a reworking of some of the older runs to give this oldest part of Breckenridge a fresh new feel.

There is equal élan down in the town, where ersatz Victorian blends with refurbished original to complete the splashiest display of architectural gingerbread in all the West. Main Street is alive with shops, restaurants, and a gaslight glow; the back streets sparkle with the historical relics that make for an interesting walking tour. Forests which surround the town literally have sprouted condominiums, most of them luxurious, enough to house more than 21,000 guests.

With such an embarrassment of riches, the break with the duplicities of the past is complete. This new Breckenridge is no sham.

Keystone, perfection in the pines

The definitive word on the status of Keystone in skiing's hierarchy came not from a mountaintop, but up out of the steam of a hot tub.

"This isn't easy for me to say because I've spent my life developing golf and tennis resorts and I'm good at it," came the visitor's velvet voice, heavy with the honeyed tones of the South. "But this is the best-run resort of any kind in the whole damned country."

It is a compliment that Keystone graciously accepts and its competitors grudgingly acknowledge. It is the nation's only five-diamond ski resort (AAA's highest rating), the most polished in all the land. Such savoir faire is the product of total management control over all facets of the operation: skiing, lodging, restaurants, and alternative recreation. This, coupled with the long-time commitment to service by the parent Ralston Purina Corporation, has made it the closest thing to perfection the ski industry has yet seen.

There are detractors, more than a few, who contend that such operational excellence is not reflected in the terrain of Keystone Mountain. This rambling, rolled-back mountain indeed has almost universally easy skiing, and for most of the skiers who come here, that is enough. It is a place to be pampered, on the mountain as well as in the restaurants and lodges.

Three seasons ago, Keystone made a bold move, if not to completely change its image, then certainly to add a new dimension to it. This supplement, in the form of a steep, challenging pyramid off the back side of the mountain called North Peak, gave Keystone instant muscle. Now there are ample precipitous plunges and sharply moguled chutes for even the most demanding skier. Expert skiers no longer have to make excuses to their friends for spending a day, or even a week, at Keystone.

North Peak also provided something else, an immediate boost in popularity that shot the resort up to number three in the nation in attendance during the 1984-85 season with more than 915,000

► *For more than four decades, Arapahoe Basin has been the epitome of excitement for expert skiers.* JEFF ANDREW/KEYSTONE RESORT

▶ *Ice skating, above, on a large, manicured lake against a scenic backdrop is one of many diversions at Keystone.*
NICHOLAS DEVORE III/PHOTOGRAPHERS ASPEN

▶ *Like most major resorts, Keystone has an active ski-touring center, with access to both maintained trails and exciting backcountry, right.*
JEFF ANDREW/KEYSTONE RESORT

lift tickets sold. Since then, the resort also has added the most extensive night skiing system in the West, lighting Keystone Mountain top to bottom, covering 40 percent of the 2,340 vertical feet of terrain. It has replaced a faltering two-year-old gondola with another which goes faster and works more smoothly, particularly in moving night skiers uphill in warmth and comfort.

The management style is direct, straightforward. If something needs tunning or fixing, the job gets done. Such policy flies in the facc of one of the more celebrated incidents in the region's history. As the story goes, a local mine owner hired a rascal named Gassy Thompson to extend his tunnel, then left for the winter. When he returned in the spring, he found the job neatly done as prescribed. Thompson eagerly accepted

his pay and left for parts unknown; only after the snow began to melt did the owner discover the ruse. Rather than tunnel *into* the mountain, Gassy had built a structure outside, then waited for the deep snow to cover his fraud.

There was a time in the first years after the ski area was begun in 1970 when anxious locals whispered about still another cruel deception involving snow. Contrary to 30-year records of ample snowfall, Keystone kept coming up with less than it needed to stay ahead of a rapidly growing horde of enthusiasts. Again, management met the problem head-on, installing the most extensive snowmaking system west of New England, a lattice of pipes and guns covering nearly the entire mountain. Now that normal snow patterns seem to have returned, there is snow aplenty.

Typically, Keystone has turned liability into asset; it now is among the first resorts in the nation to open, often as early as mid-October, and can extend its season into May.

In contrast to the glamour of modern Keystone, with its well-ordered village twinkling beside a lake alive with ice skaters, this high valley once was a hard place. Early miners labored on the brutally steep slopes and then gave romance to their endeavors with such exotic names as Argentine, Montezuma, Peru, and Chihuahua. But a group of Pennsylvanians kept it simple, calling their camp Keystone, after their home state. The name stuck for the stagecoach station down near the bottom of the valley, and this was the one chosen for the resort as well. Who ever heard of a ski area called Chihuahua?

Arapahoe Basin, a natural high

There is another place of antiquity here, a lofty realm whose history almost is one with that of Colorado skiing. Arapahoe Basin, conceived in 1946 in a mining cabin with the extraordinary name, Alhambra, has been a special place from the very beginning. It is not just that its summit, 12,450 feet at the top of the Norway lift, is the highest lift summit in North America, or that the snow which accumulates in this massive snow basin is so deep and enduring. There is a special sensation one gets up in these rocks and crags, a high alpine experience seldom found outside Europe.

It is a place of high excitement as well, with a 43 percent gradient on a remarkable bump run called Pallavicini, named after a steep chute on Grossglockner, Austria's highest mountain. There are other runs, no less imposing, scattered around the steep barrier walls that may be skied only after ski patrolmen with explosive charges blast away the danger of avalanche. Arapahoe's snow remains past the middle of June, giving it the longest season of any major area in the Rockies. Spring skiing here, with temperatures sometimes in the seventies, is one of the true delights of the sport. Beachwear predominates and the smell of tanning oil blends with wood smoke from an outdoor barbecue.

Perhaps the most remarkable thing about this basin is that it is approached from the best of all base camps. Headquarters are those same opulent lodges and restaurants of Keystone, just six miles away, truly the best of all worlds.

The legacy of the Alhambra

If the white-chinked walls of the old cabin still were standing, what tales they could tell. The story would begin at some blurred point back in the 1890s, when prospectors of even less distinct origin began the digs along a hillside in the Snake River valley of Summit County that would be known, in keeping with the exotic inclination of the time, as the Alhambra Mine.

The cabin, given the same name, was nothing much to look at, even by those meager standards. Pale logs. Squat roof. Two tiny rooms, one for eating, the other for sleeping. Still, it was sturdy enough to have endured the ravages of time and mountain weather. When Max and Edna Dercum returned to the valley after World War II, it became home.

The Dercums had been here briefly in 1941 and scarcely could wait to return. Max was a man in pursuit of skiing, and he was convinced that this was where it could, and should, be found. He had been given his first skis—an ancient pair of Northlands—in 1917 at the age of five. Wherever he went as a young man in the thirties, he left small colonies of skiers schussing in his wake.

In 1934 Dercum earned the first ski letter ever given at Cornell University before moving to Penn State University in 1936 as a professor of forestry. There he founded a ski club, fashioned

a ski hill, and not incidentally, met Edna Strand, a woman who shared his Norwegian heritage and love for skiing. After the war they returned to Colorado to continue this compulsive search for a place to build a great ski area.

Earlier, the Dercums had purchased a plot of land at the base of Keystone Mountain. Now, with such remote property deemed almost worthless, they purchased yet another tract, an old mill site at the neck of a high alpine basin on the west side of Loveland Pass. Not content, they acquired a mining patent farther up the slope.

Already forces were in motion to begin the protracted process that eventually would make Summit County the most popular ski region in the nation. Larry Jump, a former Dartmouth skier and a veteran of the Tenth Mountain Division, had been commissioned by the Denver Chamber of Commerce to locate a suitable ski area not far from the city. Jump fell in love with the huge bowl we now know as Arapahoe Basin—the very place the Dercums had bought their land.

There was a knock on the cabin door early one morning in March 1946. Still clad in pajamas, the Dercums scrambled up to greet three men. Jump had brought with him Sandy Schauffler, another ski enthusiast, and Thor Groswold, who had gained a reputation as the nation's best ski maker. When they finally left it was well into the afternoon and the Arapahoe Basin Corporation had been formed.

For the next 21 years Max Dercum was a fixture at Arapahoe, assisting in the construction of the lifts and super-

vising the ski school. But he still had not found his perfect ski mountain. All the while he had his eye on a broad, tree-thatched shoulder of Keystone Mountain, a rolling, unobtrusive hunk of national forest land certain to catch the attention of absolutely no one save the special few with keen eyes for ski terrain. Over the years Dercum skied and hiked virtually every square foot of the slope, preparing a prospectus which included his own sketches, maps, and hand-crafted models.

In 1966 he convinced the Forest Service to give him a study permit. After all those years in the closet, Dercum's dream finally was out in the open for all to see. There was just one catch. Developing such a large mountain on the scale Dercum envisioned would take money. Lots of it. Clint Murchison, Jr., the Texas oilman who already had a stake in Vail, sent lawyers to look it over. For a time, there was interest from Dave McCoy, whose Mammoth Mountain in California was then the largest ski resort in the nation. But no investment was forthcoming, and by 1968, Dercum faced the prospect of watching his permit expire. The dream was about to go down the drain.

"We had approached everyone we could think of. Nothing seemed to work," Max remembered.

It was at this low ebb that the genie of the Alhambra cabin, bottled up for more than two decades, popped out of the jar. The Dercums had sold the cabin to a sourdough, who in turn had peddled it to a group from Iowa for use as rustic, inexpensive lodging on an annual ski foray to the Rockies.

Among them was William Bergman, an attorney from Cedar Rapids, who believed in Dercum's dream and who also had powerful connections in the Midwest. This time it was Max who came calling at the Alhambra.

"Before long we thrashed the whole thing out. My spirits soared," Max recalled.

Edna had another recollection. "When we finished, we toasted our plan with a bottle of champagne. The cork went flying and landed in a light fixture. Bill Bergman kept it there for years as a memento of the occasion."

Back in Iowa, Bergman marshaled a group of associates as investors in this new ski resort. The plot thickened with the entry of another Bergman client, the giant Ralston Purina Company.

"They had the money and were looking for diversification," Bergman explained. "It simply was one of those deals which happened along at the right time for everyone."

That the plan worked and the resort prospered is a matter of record. In the 1984-85 season, its fifteenth, Keystone became the nation's third most popular ski resort, trailing only McCoy's Mammoth Mountain and Vail. Dercum's dream now is laced with lifts and trails; the meadows at the base are alive with lodges, condominiums, and restaurants.

But the Alhambra cabin no longer is nestled in the stand of lodgepole pines beneath the crags. Reclaimed by the Forest Service, it was torn down as part of a thrust to restore the area to its natural state.

When it fell, a large parcel of Colorado ski history went with it.

Copper Mountain

There is one bit of counsel that cannot be ignored by skiers traveling the I-70 corridor. It still is difficult to find a better place to ski than Copper Mountain. Even the U.S. Forest Service, a cautious bureaucracy, could not contain itself when, in a 1969 assessment, it called Copper the best yet-to-be-developed ski hill in Colorado.

"If there ever was a mountain that had terrain created for skiing, it would be Copper Mountain," the report enthused.

Certainly the fledgling area had everything anyone could imagine. Foremost was that perfectly sculpted ski terrain with a history of deep snow which surely would bring skiers running. They would not have to run far, just 75 miles west of Denver on an interstate highway with no passes to cross. Equally important for the founders, there was plenty of private land for profitable development.

But Copper Mountain, named after an abandoned turn-of-the-century copper mine near the summit, had one nagging problem: It wasn't born with a silver spoon. For a time, it didn't even have chopsticks. With an initial capitalization of just $500,000 from 16 diverse investors, management set out to do a job that demanded at least four times as much. Worse, all this happened during one of those unforeseen glitches in the economy that bordered on outright recession. Money wasn't exactly walking in off the street.

This was the task facing Charles D. "Chuck" Lewis, the former Vail executive who was hired as general managing partner. Down to his last $25,000 at one

point, Lewis finally was able to obtain the necessary financing while dealing with assorted construction problems in what might be termed an innovative fashion. To alleviate the cash crunch, Lewis started his own cement company and sawmill, not only cutting costs by more than half, but also producing enough concrete and lumber to sell on the outside market.

Still, Copper was a year behind schedule when it finally opened in the fall of 1972, a delay that, if nothing else, served to whet the appetites of skiers eager to see what all the fuss was about.

What they found was a mountain notable for the perfect order of its terrain. With few exceptions, Copper's

► An opportunity to ski untracked powder on the upper slopes of Copper Mountain, left, makes it more than worthwhile to hike up where the lifts leave off.
KAHNWEILER/JOHNSON PHOTO

► With only the mountains, the sun, and the clouds as companions, a skier tests the powder of Spaulding Bowl, above, at Copper Mountain. JEFF ANDREW/COPPER MOUNTAIN

steepest terrain is on its east side, the easiest on the west, and the intermediate in the middle. Further, it is possible to descend quickly from any direction to a common meeting place at The Center, the primary restaurant and warming house.

There was a time when it seemed The Center was too convenient a gathering point. Camaraderie also bred lift lines, a problem that first was alleviated by exciting new additions on the expert side of the mountain, then obliterated in 1986 by the resort's first superchair, the American Flyer. This strategic lift runs from The Center up 1,900 vertical feet to a place called Indian Ridge, high up near timberline, a vantage point from which skiers can scatter in all directions to all manner of terrain, including the enticing powder of Union Bowl.

The year before, the resort achieved the state's most impressive expansion with the opening of Spaulding Bowl, a double-black-diamond expanse of powder reaching above timberline to a point near the Copper Mountain summit at 12,360 feet. The bowl forms a fitting crown for four long expert runs off into the trees below, a perfect complement to a sweeping expanse of terrain outstanding in both scope and quality.

Such has not always been the case for Copper's village, whose development lagged behind the mountain until a recent surge produced a spate of restaurants and shops, along with a complete athletic club. Copper also has something unknown to any other American ski resort, its own Club Med.

The net result is a resort with a bright future, a place indeed created for skiing. Your very own Forest Service wouldn't lie to you.

Stirrings in the southwest

The mountains are bold and steep and among the most scenic in the land, and there is a certain excitement to the ski resorts of Colorado's southwest that suggests a bright future for an area time and the nation's skiers almost forgot.

One sees it first in the satiny billow of snow that piles deeper here than in any other place in the state, powder often measured in feet rather than inches. Then one hears it in the dulcet voices of the skiers, sons and daughters of a Southland which stretches from Florida to Arizona.

Part of the attraction is geographic, south to South, and it began for no more complex a reason than that it is feasible from many points along this southern tier to load up a station wagon or van and head for the slopes. The rest is shaped by marketing strategies that follow this time-honored theme: One buys—and sells—what one knows best.

It is a beneficent link that, with the spread of the skiing gospel throughout the Sunbelt, has thrust resorts like Crested Butte, Purgatory, and Telluride into greater prominence and prosperity and suddenly transformed the southwest into a hotbed of expansion. Already a permit has been issued to build a new, major resort near Wolf Creek, and yet another is planned almost in its shadow.

There also are ambitious schemes for the existing resorts, additions that finally would bring parity with those to the north. The stirrings might soon become a commotion.

The Butte is a beaut

"Ski the Great Unknown."

This promotional slogan for Crested Butte was intended to connote challenge and adventure. Alas, it proved more descriptive instead. After 26 years of siren's song aimed at luring the nation's skiers to this hideaway in the southern Colorado Rockies, the resort remains somewhat obscure against the standard of renown established by those just to the north.

▶ *Crested Butte, a favorite hangout for the wild bunch in any season, becomes a center of hang gliding excitement in summer.* DANN COFFEY/ THE STOCK BROKER

► *The snowscapes at Crested Butte are among the best in the West, a constant exhilaration for the cross-country skier.* JENNY HAGER/ ALPINE IMAGES

The reason is chiefly geographic and, for those visitors who revel in the relative seclusion of this retreat, fortuitous. Crested Butte is nestled in the ample bosom of a dead-end valley surrounded on three sides by towering mountains 28 miles north of the town of Gunnison and 230 miles from Denver and its airline hub. It is that last statistic that has been both the boon and bane of a place whose isolation from the ravening hordes along the Front Range has kept it always proud, but sometimes poor.

It would be difficult to overstate the raw charm of a town that, in contrast to most of its high-country contemporaries, has its foundations more in coal than in gold and silver. The early miners, mostly of Eastern European origin, were an unpretentious lot who produced little of the Victorian grandeur of the silver barons. What they did leave behind was an abiding sense of tranquil mountain existence, a commodity whose appeal has only heightened over the years.

This valley was the site of some of Colorado's earliest skiing around 1880 and very likely its first ski race. Since

1962, the sport has been at once the focal point of its hopes for economic revival and the epicenter of its frustrations. It must be understood in such a discussion that there are two Crested Buttes: the sometimes sleepy, always idyllic, little town of antiquity and the much newer Mount Crested Butte up the hill at the base of the distinctive mountain with the cock's comb crown. The separation between nineteenth-century town and twentieth-century ski mountain often has been greater than the intervening two miles. That they have not always pulled in the same harness is but another element in the overall struggle.

None of this should suggest that Crested Butte has not tasted success. More than 380,000 skiers passed through the turnstiles in the 1986-87 season, and its recent attendance gain has been the state's best. But resorts of similar size in the I-70 corridor west of Denver attract twice that many, nearly half of whom are day skiers from the city. Crested Butte's challenge is to make up the difference almost solely from tourists. In the past, they came mainly by auto caravan up from the South and Southwest. Now, with greatly improved air service, they are arriving on direct flights from major population centers and on commuter shuttles from the Denver airport.

Whether they continue to arrive in such growing numbers may depend upon the resort's ability to proceed with its planned North Village development, a project that not only would open an entirely separate base area of lodges and shops, but also fill what some perceive as a gnawing gap in the balance of terrain. In a sense, Crested Butte has been a mountain of extremes, with a wealth of broad, ego-pleasing runs interspersed with boots-to-the-wall black-diamond chutes. If there is a poverty here, it is the in-between. The many accomplished skiers who gravitate to the Butte now have a new T-bar to take them onto the superexpert North Face, previously accessible only to those willing to endure a 15-minute climb. These are the same daredevils who revel in the region's marvelous outback skiing and who, on a day each February, gather to contest a memorial to one of the early ski legends. The Al Johnson Uphill-Downhill salutes the old mail carrier with a race that involves first running straight uphill on skis, then schussing down the steep North Face to the finish.

But it is Mount Snodgrass, the big hummock above North Village, that will make the intermediate skier—and the cash register—chime. The holdup is cost, a minimum of $35 million for the basic groundwork, as much as $600 million for the total commercial package spread over a decade or more. Rather than make a patchwork beginning, management has elected to seek outside investors with pockets as deep as the Crested Butte powder. Against the backdrop of a static skier market and concern over the future of mountain real estate, few have been forthcoming.

Crested Butte is banking that its continued strong performance in the marketplace—abetted by a new spirit of cooperation between mountain and town, a plush resort hotel, and all those new flights arriving daily—will convince investors to reach deep. No matter. With or without North Village, Crested Butte remains a great little place well worth knowing.

► *The big cock's comb mountain which gives Crested Butte its name, top, dominates the landscape for miles around.*
DAVID SUMNER/CRESTED BUTTE MOUNTAIN RESORT

► *Skiing the high and wild, bottom, has always been a hallmark of the Crested Butte area, site of some the state's earliest skiing activity.* CRESTED BUTTE MOUNTAIN RESORT/COLORADO SKI COUNTRY USA

► *Exciting skiing and spectacular scenery are the things visitors remember most about Telluride.*
KEN GALLARD

Telluride: wild, woolly, and wonderful

Back in 1889, an ambitious young man named Butch Cassidy withdrew $24,000 from the San Miguel Valley Bank without benefit of a savings account and melted into the mountains, the first heist in the long and sporadically successful career of an outfit called the Wild Bunch.

Just two years later, a diminutive attorney with the improbable name Lucien Lucius Nunn, who may have won his law degree in a poker game, made the world's first long-distance transmission of alternating current, and Telluride soon laid claim to being the best-lighted town in the nation. It was here, after the collapse of the silver market, that presidential candidate William Jennings Bryan delivered his "Cross of Gold" speech in 1903 on a bunting-clad platform by the steps of the Sheridan Hotel, just a few paces from the opera

► *A Christmas away from home still can be festive with a spread like this one, far left, at a Telluride restaurant.* KEN GALLARD

► *Telluride's rustic Gorrono Ranch Restaurant, left, situated halfway up the ski slopes, commands one of the grander views in ski country.* KEN GALLARD

house where Sarah Bernhardt, Lillian Gish, and Lillian Russell performed. Socialist Eugene Victor Debs also came here to rail against the plight of the mine workers, and following bloody strikes, union president Charles Moyer was held prisoner for six months by the National Guard in an upstairs room of the sumptuous Sheridan.

Nothing much had happened in Telluride since these turn-of-the-century fireworks until a Los Angeles attorney named Joseph Zoline, who previously had demonstrated his willingness to gamble by breeding racehorses, decided to roll the dice on a ski resort. It may be argued that in the 15 years since that 1971 opening, the pace didn't accelerate much. Despite a marvelous ski moun-tain, a spectacular natural setting, and what may be the most rustically charming of all mountain towns, Telluride wasn't exactly overrun with visitors.

The reason is isolation, the very quality that made it the favorite sixties hangout for the counterculture crowd fleeing the citification of Aspen. Telluride is a circuitous 335-mile drive from Denver, and until 1985, the nearest air terminal was 67 miles away at Montrose with infrequent flight schedules. To ski at Telluride, no matter how desirable, it was necessary to pass over a lot of places with names like Aspen, Vail, and Steamboat.

Even with the opening of an airport just four miles outside town, Telluride attendance lags behind every other Col-orado destination resort. Those who haven't taken the extra effort to get there might be surprised at what they're missing.

For years, a weathered sign on a low wooden post just outside town pro-claimed this "The most beautiful spot on earth." No one objected. Telluride, the town, is set in a box canyon surrounded on two sides by some of the steepest and most visually imposing mountains in Colorado, giant cliff sides that leak waterfalls and put cramps in the necks of tourists. On the third is the steep north face of the ski area, whose runs have names like The Plunge and Spiral Stairs and whose extreme tilt is enough to encourage timid skiers to take the long way back to town.

As splendid as this view may be, it is not enough to detract from the allure of the town itself, whose name is taken from the binary compound tellurium, which usually contains a metal. In the Telluride district, that metal frequently was silver. Before skiing arrived, this was mountain rustic at its finest, a time warp that showed latecomers the Aspen of the forties, Breckenridge in the fifties. From the Victorian gingerbread of the old houses to the brick-and-stone citadels of the 1887 courthouse and the New Sheridan Hotel, replacing the original which burned, the place was magic.

Now the look has changed, perhaps for the better. The old buildings still are there, but with the jaunty air that comes from a fresh coat of paint and a new roof. Moreover, Telluride has been proclaimed a national historic district, which mandates that all new structures conform to a strict code for replicating the traditional architectural styles. Ramshackle storefronts have been made over to highlight enticing shops, palate-pleasing restaurants, and still-rowdy bars.

While Telluride's newcomers include the usual battery of real-estate rogues, coupon clippers, and not a few refugees from the glitter of celebrity, it retains a certain frontier blush which only embellishes the appeal. But nothing of the modern Telluride matches its past, when conductors on the old Rio Grande Southern narrow-gauge railroad signaled the train's approach by bellowing, somewhat prophetically, "To hell you ride!" Or when, in 1900, the town clerk answered the query of a Boston woman about the state of Telluride society with this synopsis:

"As for sowciety, it is bang up. This is a mighty morrel town, considerin that theres 39 saloons and two newspapers in a poppylation of 4,247. But every saloon has a sine up sayin that all fitin must be done outside. Only two men has been killed since Monday and termoroer will be Wednesday. Don't hezzytate about coming here on account of sowciety. This is a morrel town."

By comparison, the recent political tiffs between the Telluride Company (Tellco) and local businessmen have been tame. The company is the developer of the ski slopes and, more recently, a four-season resort village at the base of the lifts. Residents of the town protested that the new mountain complex would pull people away from their shops. Peace of sorts has broken out, largely because Tellco has promised to build an interconnecting gondola and because everyone is excited at the prospect of new prosperity fueled by the airport and ski improvements. Among the investors moving in is the great Austrian downhill racer Franz Klammer, whose lodge will be a centerpiece of the new village.

Telluride long ago earned its stripes among expert skiers for such things as the 3,105-vertical-foot, straight-shot challenges of The Plunge and Spiral Stairs, the longest and steepest trails in all the land. Then there's the equally steep glade skiing off the Apex lift at the top of the main area, the powder chutes to the south, and a host of other runs which would be stars in a lesser firmament. Beginners also have been cheered by the broad, flat runs at the bottom, but it has been the relative dearth of in-between terrain that may be the primary factor in muting the chimes of the cash register. This ill now has been cured with the 1986 installation of North America's longest superchair. The Sunshine Express travels more than two miles and 1,800 vertical feet to reach a broad new swatch of intermediate terrain which completes the picture. There's another, equally pleasing element to Telluride skiing. With lodging for just 3,000 and a mountain capacity more than twice that, one can be reasonably assured of not being held up—either in a bank or a lift line.

Purgatory, a solace for lost souls

Early Spanish explorers, frustrated by the hellish tangle of its rocky gorges, called it *El Rio de las Animas Perdidas en Purgatorio*, River of Lost Souls in Purgatory.

In addition to the inference of torturous travel, the name also suggests that something very hot is not far away. So it is that Purgatory Resort, which traded on the name of the nearby river for dramatic effect, can claim one devilish advantage over the frozen ski palaces to the north. Just an hour's drive from the rim of the great southwest desert, Purgatory offers the comforts of improved weather without sacrificing the quality of snow. More warmth, more sun, more snow. Is it any wonder so many from the even warmer climes to the south and west make this their ski resort of choice?

There is much more to Purgatory than balmy temperatures and some of the best powder in the state. There is an equally attractive mountain, tilted toward the middle-ability range, with plenty of room to roam. Still, this

► *Purgatory's run Catharsis is therapeutic only for experts.*
DIRK GALLIAN

▶ *Ample new luxury lodging right at the base of the mountain is one sign of bold expansion at Purgatory.*
KEN GALLARD

remains an inconspicuous place. Despite a recent flurry of development, including a new spur to the ski slopes, a shopping complex, and a number of posh condos, the gait is slow and easy; this is not skiing's fast lane.

Part of the reason is location. Although there is commuter air service 44 miles from the ski area, the vast majority of skiers drive up from Texas, New Mexico, and Arizona. The setting is rustic, with something of an Old West air. The feeling begins in Durango, a city of 18,000 just 28 miles to the south, which forms the gateway to the ski resort and also catches its lodging overflow. Durango is, in addition, a portal to Mesa Verde National Park, a strategic location that brings in waves of summer visitors. The motels built to hold them provide a less expensive lodging alternative for skiers on a budget.

There is much to see on the drive up from Durango to the resort. The road climbs past a broad meadow where a wintering herd of elk blows frosty breath into the air. At a place where the highway leaves the Animas River valley and winds upward through thick groves of oakbrush and aspen, thermal hot pots bubble up from the bowels of the the earth. The thought occurs that those old Spaniards had a better insight into the true nature of the place than one might have imagined.

There are all manner of surprises here, not the least of which comes at a sharp bend that nearly hides the companion resort of Tamarron, a separate conglomeration of townhouses and hotel rooms that, with room for 1,200 guests, remains Purgatory's primary lodging base. Then, nearer the ski area,

► *La Plata Mountains, near Purgatory, are favored by winter ski campers for enticing terrain and deep snow. An increasing number of hardy outdoor enthusiasts think little of spending a winter night out under the stars.*
STEWART AITCHISON

the foothills to the east part to reveal one of the most stunning sights in all the Rockies, the ragged spires of the San Juan Needles.

Finally, there is the resort itself. With the sudden sprouting of several condominiums around a new Village Center, the first stages of a planned $250 million leap into the big time, the face of Purgatory has changed. In place of the backwoods past, there now is a kind of understated luxury, efficient and comfortable without being gaudy. More than one happy refugee has described it as much like the better resorts of New England, only with more snow and better weather.

This is a skier's mountain, broad-shouldered and roomy. It is the kind that swallows you up, lures you ever deeper into its mysteries. One does not master it in a day or two or three. Because it has such a reputation for powder and because there isn't always a snow machine poised to pounce on every flake that falls, Purgatory has been considered a haven for expert skiers. Part of this respect comes from the initial impression left by those

first-developed slopes just above the village, a staircase of steep steps with names that leave nothing—and everything—to the imagination.

Runs like Lower Hades, Pandemonium, Styx, and a quick, mean little plunge called 666 get your attention even before you climb on the lift. But once past these, a skier also finds trails with names like Cherub, Mercy, Paradise, and Angel's Tread to quiet any nerves that might have been overly jangled by the imposing face.

Beyond these, Purgatory rambles along through a seemingly endless expanse of intermediate terrain, some of it in broad, open trails, the rest running wild in a labyrinth of glades in which the powder seems to last forever.

More recently, the resort opened an entirely new sweep of territory, 125 acres in all, for advanced and intermediate skiers, called The Legends, named after ski pioneers who helped build the resort.

Purgatory offers a number of diversions you'll not find at any other resort. The ride on the historic narrow-gauge railroad from Durango to Silverton up through a part of the San Juan Mountains, which may be Colorado's most spectacular, is even more scenic in winter. In another direction lie the cliff dwellings of Mesa Verde National Park and, in between, the separate wonders of old Durango, with its registered National Historic District.

If this is Purgatory, punish us more.

In praise of all things small

In a different setting, it would be a star. From its lofty perch astride a massive snow basin, the ski area can speak of one of the nation's longest seasons, October to May, with outstanding snow and a fine variety of trails scattered over a 1,430-foot vertical drop. Powder conditions are common, lifts run smoothly, service is friendly, and the largest population center in all the Rockies is just 56 miles of interstate away, with no passes to cross. History runs deep here. Colorado skiers have been climbing up into this timberline realm for more than a half-century. Organized skiing dates back almost to World War II.

Yet in the exceedingly fast lane that is the ski corridor immediately west of Denver, Loveland Basin is but a bit player in a very large production, a member of the chorus behind star performers like Vail, Winter Park, and Ski the Summit. The trouble is not the slopes or the snow or even the access. Rather it is that Loveland is located exclusively on national forest land and has only limited base-area development: no slopeside lodging, no discos, no French restaurants.

Almost precisely the same is true at Monarch and Wolf Creek. Both have splendidly varied terrain with exceptional snow, but the great masses of skiers somehow manage to pass them by in favor of the gloss and glitter of the larger resorts. Ski Cooper, the precise spot high on Tennessee Pass where the

► *Made famous in song and prized by skiers for the deepest snow in the state, the Wolf Creek Pass area has a rugged charm. With one existing ski area and two others in various planning stages, it also might become a focal point of the sport.*
KEN GALLARD

► Berthoud Pass with its wide-open timberline skiing has a special place in Colorado ski lore. The world's first double chair lift was installed here in 1947, and the ski area celebrated its fiftieth season of operation in 1987. ROBERT BASSE

► *Monarch ski area, located near the crest of a high mountain pass, is noted for its bounty of snow.* MONARCH SKI RESORT/ COLORADO SKI COUNTRY USA

Tenth Mountain troops placed their training lift, keeps running year to year chiefly for the benefit of the neighboring communities. Each of these smaller areas manages to survive well enough, fed by skiers either drawn to the intimate atmosphere or wooed by prices substantially below their larger neighbors. The same basic realities exist at Ski Broadmoor, Conquistador, Cuchara Valley, Ski Estes Park, Powderhorn, St. Mary's Glacier, SilverCreek, and Ski Sunlight—all clinging to niches of varying dimensions in the shadow of giants.

There are other, more telling, indicators of the plight of small areas. Berthoud Pass, that lofty old area just 57 miles from Denver where the world's first double chair lift was strung in 1947, barely sells more lift tickets in an entire season than the 14,000 to 15,000 tickets Vail sells on one good day. Collectively, Colorado's 20 or so small areas do not match the season atten-

dance of one Breckenridge. Further, recent trends look no more promising. There have been six Colorado closures in the last half-decade; some areas have not reopened. Nationally, the number of ski areas has shrunk from about a thousand in the mid-seventies to approximately 700 today. The attrition has been almost exclusively from the ranks of the little guys.

The reasons for the decline often are subtle, but sometimes as blunt as the $175,000 cost of a grooming machine or the expense of a million or more for an entire snowmaking system. More than anything, it is that the skiers who grew up with these smaller areas two or three decades ago are either leaving the sport or have gone off to the sparkle of the big resorts, never to return.

The trend is nettlesome not only to the smaller areas and the skiers who love them, but also to the industry as a whole. For it is these low-cost areas that

traditionally have served as skiing's cradle, that have taught the children, that have in a very real way served as a recruiting ground for the entire sport.

The reason to like these smaller ski areas is for themselves, for their down-home intimacy, for the personal touch. You can find the president of the company on the other side of an open door, and the guy running the lift will remember that he saw you last week. You'll leave with more friends than you came with.

More than anything, you'll learn that, even in an era when everything is measured rather than savored, size isn't everything. Shakespeare said it best in *As You Like It*, when Jacques asked Orlando of his lady fair, "What stature is she of?"

Orlando's reply was spoken for everyone who loves a small ski area: "Just as high as my heart."

► *A backcountry skier kicks off a cornice above the Red Lady Bowl on Mount Emmons, just above the town of Crested Butte, to start an avalanche that will stablize the snowpack below.* GARY SPRUNG/GNURPS

Orphaned Little Annie, Adam's missing rib, and other tales from Colorado Ski Country

It was the ski area that had everything—great figure, good looks, charm, style, lineage, and suitors lined up for blocks. Even had a Broadway play named after it.

Trouble was, there was no Daddy Warbucks in real life, no Punjab to protect it. So what we have now, high atop the Colorado Rockies, is another ski resort on the skids, homeless, at least temporarily abandoned. Orphaned Little Annie.

It is a popular misconception that every ski resort is a success, particularly in that most desirable of all locations, Colorado. Yet even here, adverse economic factors have in recent years pulled down what seemed otherwise sound endeavors. Such was the case of Little Annie, which would have been Aspen's fifth major ski area had not the magic money carpet flown away.

There also were big plans for Rifle, but, again, the developers were forced to bite the bullet when shale oil went on the rocks. The troubles have not been quite so clearly defined at Adam's Rib, which, 17 years and millions of dollars after its first permit application, still is alive and kicking, but perhaps no nearer completion.

Building a ski resort, especially a large one, is no simple matter. Everyone knows it takes money. Lots of money. What is less understood is the incredible snarl of bureaucracy—reports stacked on top of statements piled upon permits— that can delay even the best-heeled and most desirable project all the way to its grave.

For every Vail, which sped quickly along to its destiny as America's largest single ski resort, there is a Beaver Creek, which, despite the total backing of the rich Vail parent, nearly strangled on red tape. For every Aspen, a Little Annie.

The culprits come in strange and mysterious forms—everything from the fiscal policies of the Mitterand government in France to the price of oil in Saudi Arabia to good old made-in-the-USA interest rates. Whatever the causes, the result has been the same: the demise of a number of planned major ski resorts. This shouldn't suggest that the industry has crouched into a terminal snowplow. There are two new projects well along in the Wolf Creek Pass area near Pagosa Springs, another being pushed near Leadville. But compared with the spate of construction that brought us Snowmass, Keystone, Copper Mountain, and Mary Jane inside of a decade, recent movement has come at a glacial pace.

Apart from escalating construction costs and bureaucratic delays, other factors have worked against new development. One is that all the existing resorts have accomplished dramatic expansion, sucking up skier growth that more recently has slowed dramatically. Now that national skier numbers have leveled off, it seems far less attractive to risk the millions required to compete in an increasingly competitive market. There can be no more pipe dreams of buying into this exclusive club cheaply. Against the backdrop of such demands, there's little wonder that some projects have wound up with long expectations and short pockets.

There can be no better example than Little Annie, named after the silver mine up on Richmond Hill that took its name from the miner's daughter who often was seen picking wildflowers in the alpine meadows high above Aspen. Almost from the times when adventurers climbed with seal skins up these slopes, skiers have been fascinated by this boundless, gladed terrain just off the eastern shoulder of Aspen Mountain.

A few years ago, fascination turned to unabashed love. Longtime Aspen resident Dave Farney formed a development group that quickly won the hearts of skiers and local government alike. Aspen had been lagging at the box office, and Annie, with enough gorgeous intermediate terrain hanging right there above town to swallow two areas the size of Snowmass, was just the ticket to revitalization. But even with this kind of endorsement, there were pitfalls. For Little Annie it was a deadly combination of growing expenses and shrinking finances. Investors simply did not have the money. Rescue might have come from a source stranger than anything in the comics or even on Broadway. However, a partnership loan from Les Arcs, a resort in the French Alps, fell through when Mitterand's socialists halted the flow of francs outside the country. By the time Farney's fingers reached the bottom of his pockets, $3.6 million had been exhausted. So, too, had the will to continue.

See you in the funny papers.

An equally unique fate jammed the firing mechanism at Rifle, a planned destination resort located near a town of the same name on the westernmost fringe of the I-70 ski corridor. Part of the ammunition for this large development was to have been a local population explosion fueled by a neighboring synthetic petroleum boom. But a stagnant international market pulled the plug on shale oil, and any interest in investing in a nearby ski area leaked away with it.

Even more frustrating is the situation at Adam's Rib, conceived as a giant, four-season resort on the southwestern rim of the Eagle Valley, not far from Vail and Beaver Creek. Mount Adam is not without appeal: 3,300 vertical feet of outstanding terrain; room for 17 chair lifts, a gondola, and 9,000 skiers; a village plan for 15,000 beds, monorail, and two golf courses. There even is a Mount Eve next door with whom to chew the old apple. In marked contrast to Little Annie and Rifle, Adam's Rib also has an Eden of financial support.

What it doesn't have, what has kept it snakebit for 17 years, are the reams of permits needed to proceed. Lawsuits by environmentalists, local opposition, waffling by the U.S. Forest Service—all have conspired to keep it from blooming. The developer keeps pushing ahead, but there's no telling where, or when, the path will end.

There is a cruel fiscal reality in any dream of starting a new ski resort these days. Jim Branch, president of Sno-Engineering/Resource Management, the nation's largest ski consulting firm, is brutally realistic about the matter.

"We tell our clients if they don't have at least $20 million for the first phase of the development, they shouldn't jump. We advise them to stick their toe in first or look for a more shallow pool."

Despite such demands and odds, there still are developers out there with a dream—all waiting, all watching millions in seed money evaporate with each successive delay. Deep in every heart is the hope that tomorrow is only a day away.

► *The Colorado Rockies support the state's second-largest income source after agriculture.*
CRAIG AURNESS/WEST LIGHT

A new day for the old way

A renaissance in cross-country skiing

At the start of it all, nobody skied for fun. Certainly that is the presumption of ethnologists who have delved into peat bogs across Scandinavia and pulled out the conclusion that skiing originated as early as 5,000 years ago. Skis with upturned tips and leather-thong bindings, not dissimilar to the ones used earlier in this century, have been accurately dated to 500 B.C. For these hardy Norsemen, the necessity of traveling across a landscape covered by snow much of the year was the mother of this invention. That they became instruments of war and hunting and, invariably, of the sport—the biathlon—which mimics those activities, was inevitable. It is more than coincidence that Ullr, the Scandinavian god of winter, always is portrayed on skis with curved toes.

Perhaps the best record of the military use of skis is from the battle of Oslo about A.D. 1200, when King Sverre of Norway dispatched scouts across the snow to spy on the hated Swedes. Just six years later, during a subsequent civil war, the king sent two skiers, who wrapped their legs in birch bark against the cold, to carry his infant son through the mountains to safety. Today, Norwegians celebrate the event with an annual Birkebeinerrennet, or "birch-leg" race, over the same 35-mile course of antiquity.

Similarly, the Swedes celebrate the flight of a sixteenth-century patriot, Gustav Vasa, to rally his countrymen against the Danes. The modern Vasaloppet, a faithful 53 miles, attracts tens of

► *Copper Mountain powder, far left, provides a perfect playground for executing telemark turns.*
JEFF ANDREW/COPPER MOUNTAIN

► *Blowing snow can't deter backcountry skiers inching toward the top of Pearl Pass, left, both a winter connection between Aspen and Crested Butte and a favored place for cruising down vast snowfields.*
JENNY HAGER/ALPINE IMAGES

thousands of racers each year. Both of these ancient events have been replicated with enthusiasm in the United States among skiers who increasingly have adopted the old ways as best.

As recently as three decades ago, cross-country skiing in this country was something of a novelty practiced chiefly by nostalgic Scandinavian descendants and a few hardy mountain residents who embraced it as part of a rustic lifestyle. Instead, the more glamorous "alpine" adaptation of the sport, a product of experimentation in Austria around the turn of the century, took North America by storm.

Ironically, it was during the peak of America's alpine boom, in the late sixties and seventies, that ski touring, the art of traveling across the countryside on narrow skis with loose-heel bindings, began to blossom. The reasons for this renaissance are several: a

▶ *Citizen touring races, characterized by every-man-for-himself mass starts such as this one at Snowmass, far left, became popular in the late sixties and remain high spots on the nordic calendar of many mountain towns.*
WILSON GOODRICH/TOM STACK & ASSOCIATES

▶ *Double poling with strong kick and glide, left, is the classic way for a cross-country racer to accelerate on a flat surface.* DOUG LEE/TOM STACK & ASSOCIATES

▶ *The exercise is telemarking; the place is Taylor Pass, right, part of the limitless high country that makes the Crested Butte area a center of the high and the wild.* JENNY HAGER/ALPINE IMAGES

disaffection with lift lines, a minor rebellion against the expense of alpine equipment and lift tickets, a protest against the perceived snobbishness of alpinists, and a sense of freedom from the madding crowd. But it is equally likely that the touring boom merely was an outgrowth of the same fitness craze which filled our paths with joggers, a back-to-nature binge born of the urge to continue running outdoors in winter and of the convenience of being able to go touring wherever there is snow.

This trend was not lost on ski resorts, which scrambled to establish touring centers complete with many miles of prepared track as a means of keeping in touch with this fast-growing segment of the sport. Partly as a result, there evolved a broad middle ground of all-around skiers who are equally at home on the flat and on the steep.

It is an equal irony that from this fusion of interest came yet another of those curious returns to roots, the telemark, a highly stylized turn that originated in the region of southern Norway of the same name. This most graceful of skiing maneuvers resembles nothing quite so much as a curtsy with a deep knee bend that thrusts the lead, or steering, ski far out in front while the rear ski provides edge control. By necessity, it is performed on touring gear with a loose heel, but generally with the addition of a metal edge on the ski. Other popular modifications include a stiff high-top boot, sometimes converted from an old leather alpine boot, for better control. With these modern adaptations, accomplished telemarkers can negotiate any terrain, from the meanest moguls to the most prodigious powder.

Out of the telemark revival, which sprouted among young enthusiasts at Crested Butte, has come what might be considered a separate sport within a sport. It is called, in the national penchant for amalgamation, norpine, a marriage of nordic and alpine, and means using nordic equipment to ski downhill. Practitioners have little difficulty detailing the attraction: a break in the normal routine of skiing, a greater challenge, a heightened sense of style.

► *Dream Lake, in Rocky Mountain National Park, seems a fitting name for an other-worldly ski touring scene.* KENT & DONNA DANNEN

At the cutting edge of this activity is a daredevil band of adventurers whose greatest satisfaction comes in transporting themselves by helicopter, snowcat, or sheer muscle power to some distant snowfield where the only track is from a snowshoe hare and the only sound is the soft hiss of powder snow beneath a fast ski.

If they use nordic gear, they may traverse their way straight up the slope. If the run will be made on alpine equipment, the skiers must either ride up or carry their gear on their backs. Such sport is either highly expensive or brutally difficult. In the main, those who choose it are the elite, skilled skiers for whom the joys of communing with this winter wilderness are worth any price or risk.

Against the dramatic backdrop of such adventuring, it is easy to understate the impact of the type of skiing the old Norsemen had in mind at the very start of it all. Whether the call is nature or fitness, an increasing number of winter recreationists are taking their sport on relatively flat terrain using narrow skis with loose-heel bindings.

On a weekend morning, they may be found streaming up from Denver on I-70 or any number of secondary routes, cross-country skis conspicuously attached to roof-top racks. Often these racks contain a mixture of gear, a validation of the earlier judgment by all of Colorado's major resorts to provide a variety of experiences for their guests. Without exception, these ski areas painstakingly maintain extensive loops of trails, often ten miles or more, and operate separate touring centers, complete with rentals and instruction.

Other centers have evolved at guest ranches or summer lodges eager for some form of income to assuage the cold-weather doldrums. Here, the attraction is companionship with kindred spirits in a setting at once rustic and comfortable—perhaps as close to the concept of the communal ski lodge of a half-century ago as one can find.

But for reasons of economy or freedom, most tourers prefer simply to strike out on their own. In a place of such mountain abundance, there is no shortage of opportunity. Nearly every valley forms a contoured ski route: a gentle climb along a stream tinkling beneath its icy mantle, a spirited glide back down on glazed tracks. There is scarcely a mountain town of substance that does not include a shop which dispenses both touring gear and guidebooks to neighboring trails.

These wide-open spaces may be as tame as an alpine meadow or as spectacular as a glacial gorge. The ultimate beauty of it all is that the skier gets to choose. ∎

▶ *At 12,930 feet elevation, Sunshine Peak, top, dwarfs a solitary skier in the San Miguel Mountains of southwest Colorado.* ROBERT BASSE

▶ *An excellent form of exercise, ski touring is a delightful entrée to the winter out-of-doors for people of all ages, bottom left.* NICHOLAS DEVORE III / PHOTOGRAPHERS ASPEN

▶ *Much is made of the solitude ski touring can afford. But it can be just as much fun in a group, bottom right.* GRAFTON MARSHALL SMITH/BRECKENRIDGE SKI AREA

▶ *The Sawatch Range, which contains the tallest mountains in Colorado, offers a bounty of wilderness snowscapes.* SPENCER SWANGER/TOM STACK & ASSOCIATES

Neither rain nor snow . . .

On a warm, moonlit night in March, a man on skis leaves the dim lights of Breckenridge behind and makes his way up the Blue River valley toward Hoosier Pass and beyond that the flat expanse of South Park. Three miles upstream, the quiet is shattered by the sound of wolves howling very near.

In his published account of the incident, the skier recalled, "I was not armed, but I was not disturbed. It was not likely, I thought, that the Good Lord would let anything disturb a man going in the night to His appointment."

Thus began another in the long series of transmountain adventures of Father John Lewis Dyer, the snowshoe itinerant. The year was 1863, 11 months after Dyer had answered the dual call of the Methodist Church and the Rocky Mountains to become a circuit minister. Dyer's pulpit was wherever he could draw a crowd among rough miners working such camps as Buckskin Joe, Montgomery, Mosquito, Fairplay, Tarryall, and California Gulch.

In winter his sole means of reaching these remote outposts was his pair of 11-foot-long skis, "Norwegian snowshoes," brought to the gold camps some years earlier by miners of Scandinavian ancestry.

Heavy and unwieldy, they nonetheless were the most efficient way of moving over snow drifted deep enough to founder a horse inside a few yards.

Well past his fiftieth birthday, Dyer quickly sized up the situation and with the demands of his first winter fast approaching, made his first pair of skis. Early on, the good father learned the same jarring reality that sooner or later confronts every beginning skier. Dyer, who had not embraced the art of hyperbole which infests modern ski biographies, wrote simply:

"On one occasion I was going down the mountain to Gold Run and my shoes got crossed in front of me, so I was going very fast. A little pine tree was right in my course and I could not turn and dared not encounter the tree with the shoes crossed. And so I threw myself into the snow and went out of sight."

With a courage rare even in a time when acts of bravery, or at least bravado, were commonplace, Dyer routinely carried the gospel across the highest mountain passes in the state, fair weather or foul. At elevations above 13,000 feet in the dead of winter, there was little fair weather to be found.

Dyer's diary is full of matter-of-fact accounts of these perilous crossings through mountains that later would become the ski playgrounds of Summit County, of storms so severe that direction became meaningless and survival a matter of raw determination. More than once he rescued stranded miners who, but for Dyer's prodding, surely would have perished.

On one occasion, it was Dyer who narrowly survived. An account in his biography, *Snowshoe Itinerant*, first published in 1890, is a study of the perils attendant to his task.

"I left California Gulch about the middle of March. It was thawing, with alternate snow and sunshine, until about one o'clock. . . .Within a few hundred feet of the pass at the end of Evans Gulch, I looked to the north and saw a black cloud just coming over. No pen or tongue can describe its awful appearance.

"I tied up my neck and ears and took my bearings . . .so that I might keep my course in the snow. But when the storm struck me, I could not have stood up had I not braced against my snowshoes, which I had taken off and held in position for that purpose.

"I found myself unable to make more than 50 yards before resting and had to hold my hand over my mouth and nose to keep the snow out so I could breathe, bracing with my snow-shoes in order to stand. On the west side, the snow blew off so that I had to carry my shoes. About the third stop, I came to a large rock and braced against it; and in the midst of the awful surround-ings, poured out my soul to God for help, and felt encouraged to try, in His name, to make the trip.

"I could not travel against the wind, so I had to bear right, which brought me on the range south of the old Indian trail, where there was no way to get down without going over a precipice. . .I had gone scarcely three rods when my foot slipped off the precipice. . .I could not tell whether the pitch was 10 feet or 50. The cold wind seemed to be feeling for my heart-strings, and my only chance for life was to let myself go over. . . .

"I said, 'O God, into Thy hands I commit my soul, my life, my all; my faith looks up to Thee,' and then, with composure, I let go and, as might be expected, there was a great body of new, soft snow for me to fall in. I have never been certain how far it was. It was soon over and I was buried in six or eight feet of new snow. . . .

"My heels struck the old snow, which must have pitched at an angle of more than 45 degrees, and my weight carried me. . .and I went at railroad speed."

Dyer survived to reach his cabin at the bottom of Mosquito Creek and resume what had become a second occupation. In addition to transporting faith across the range, he also carried the mail. In mid-winter 1893, the penniless pastor got a contract to carry the post once a week from Buckskin Joe to Cache Creek by way of Oro—a distance of 37 miles. He crossed the treacherous Mosquito Range on skis every week, delivering three sermons at mining camps along the way. Dyer was paid $18 for his mail deliveries, but soon expanded this service to include an express business carrying gold dust to ex-change for greenbacks, stuffing it all into a pack which now weighed 30 pounds or more.

In his later tenure, Dyer ranged far to the south, settling briefly in Santa Fe, New Mexico, and preaching for a time in El Paso, Texas. Appointed to the Brecken-ridge circuit in 1879, he returned to his beloved mountains of Summit County until his retirement in 1888 at the age of 76.

More than a hundred years later, only the barest skeletons of the old mining camps remain. A cabin here, a rotted foundation there, the yellow-streaked residue of tailings farther up the hill. But in Breckenridge, the spirit of the old itinerant lives on in the church he dedicated and helped build.

On your next visit, stop by the Father Dyer United Methodist Church. Go to the window, look up at the mountains and close your eyes. Imagine a dim figure under a bulky pack on long skis just breaking over the top of the range, gliding, gliding out of the past.

► *Mail carrier on skis.* COURTESY, COLORADO HISTORICAL SOCIETY F-7467

► *Who gets to play in all that water once the snow melts? The Slaughterhouse Rapids on the Colorado River, left, is a fitting challenge for kayaking, a sport that has experienced a dramatic increase in popularity.* DIRK GALLIAN

► *Snow on the high peaks, green of the golf course at the Snowmass Club, top right. Such are the delightful contrasts of the high country.* KAHNWEILER/JOHNSON PHOTO

► *Where to now? Four-wheel-drive enthusiasts, bottom right, survey the possiblities on the north end of the Gore Range.* DAVID LOKEY/VAIL-BEAVER CREEK

► Colorado's fastest-growing sport isn't skiing. Instead, it's river rafting, top left, an activity that reaches its peak in May and June amid the torrent of snowmelt. DAVID LOKEY/VAIL-BEAVER CREEK

► The water is cold, but the sailboard action is hot at Ruedi Reservoir, top right, not far from Aspen. KAHNWEILER/JOHNSON PHOTO

► A meadow near Vail, bottom right, that might have borne the imprint of cross-country ski tracks in winter has a different purpose when the seasons are reversed. DAVID LOKEY/VAIL-BEAVER CREEK

Back to the future

Planning, expansion, and reality

If that ski trail winding through the central Rockies and the theme of this book had followed the course Fritz Benedict originally intended, it would have skulked up on Vail from the rear, through that remarkable sweep of treeless powder snow known simply as the Back Bowls. A visitor from an earlier time, even as recently as a year ago, would be stupefied by the scene unfolding before him.

Here, in a wild place seemingly disconnected from the bustle and refinement on the other side of the mountain, Vail again is on the march. Under a plan approved in 1986 by the U.S. Forest Service, four lifts could be installed immediately across this grand expanse, increasing Vail's daily capacity from 15,570 skiers to 20,000. Then, if a second phase is approved, another four lifts might be added, and the capacity would skyrocket to 25,000.

But this is nothing compared with other plans being made at Vail and what is happening at a half-dozen other major resorts elsewhere in Colorado. With a few more lifts sprinkled here and there, Vail could wedge yet another 25,000 skiers into the vastness which is China, Siberia, Teacup, and Two Elks bowls, as well as on the broad ridge to the south. It is not outside the realm of possibility that, decades from now, Vail might spawn another separate village in the next valley over toward Leadville, a move that would create the largest ski complex in the world. Nor is this long-range potential limited just to Vail

► *Cornices, the product of snow, wind, and steep slopes, provide a special challenge for daredevil skiers, far left.* DAVID LOKEY/VAIL-BEAVER CREEK

► *Vail's Prima Cornice, left, is an extraordinary showcase for a skier with the right stuff.*
DAVID LOKEY/VAIL-BEAVER CREEK

► *A chair lift ride at Breckenridge can be much more than just another trip to the top of a ski run.*
BRECKENRIDGE SKI AREA

proper. At Beaver Creek capacity exists under the existing permit to expand from the present 8,000 skiers to nearly 20,000.

There also is talk, whispers that have grown louder, of yet another link on the front side, in the I-70 corridor, that would push Vail westward in a European-style lift interconnection with Beaver Creek and beyond. In a twist of fate that spans many years and even more history, the western terminal might encompass a budding independent resort called Arrowhead, whose president is Peter Seibert, the very man who started Vail 25 years ago.

Occurrences at Vail always seem bigger than life, but there are stirrings of almost equal magnitude among its neighbors. At the other end of our trail, Aspen officials are awaiting permit approval for a development on Burnt Mountain that would make Snowmass half again as large as its present 1,500 acres. Winter Park is in the process of doubling its size to 1,700 acres within a decade, a gait that could move it to the top of the heap if Vail's pace is not equally brisk. Breckenridge, which occupies three separate mountains, could claim a fourth peak. Steamboat is contemplating a leap across the valley to a separate, steeper slope called Catamount. Crested Butte is pressing to open its North Village. These are but the more dramatic alternatives. Every major resort has some expansion close at hand.

Then there are the advanced and aggressive plans for new resorts. Adam's Rib, not far from the present head of the Tenth Mountain Trail, has been waiting in the wings for years, and similar groundwork has been prepared for two major ski complexes near Wolf Creek Pass.

▶ At Breckenridge, snowmobile rides, far left, on several forest trails and high passes are a means of leaving the resort's ski slopes behind, at least for a few hours. BRECKENRIDGE SKI AREA

▶ Cold night air and high elevation make skiing Winter Park powder, left, a real breakthrough. ROD WALKER/ WINTER PARK

All this comes hard on the heels of a recent flurry of expansion to existing resorts that totals $250 million in mountain improvements alone over the last five years, a clear indication that Colorado fully intends to remain in the vanguard. But as imposing as this compendium of on-slope development may be, it pales when compared with the estimated $5 billion that has been invested in all aspects of Colorado skiing.

Such an enormous endowment of lifts, trails, lodges, restaurants, and utilities has left these resorts collectively without peer on this continent. But even as the buildup continues at a frenzied pace, a storm is brewing over these mountains, a tempest that brings us to the very heart of this trilogy of Colorado skiing: what was, what is, and

what will be. Suspicion persists that these resorts already may be overbuilt, and even the managers who have been pushing fastest are openly troubled about the future.

The reasons are as plain as the realities which tell us that national skier attendance has been stagnant at around 52 million annual visits since 1980, that the skier population has grown older, that there is increasing consumer resistance to higher prices, that new tax laws might stifle investment in mountain real estate, that the frenzy of discount air fares may be over, and that competition from alternative winter vacations in the tropics has become more intense.

Curiously, it is Vail's owner who expresses the most concern over this seeming conflict of forces. George Gil-

lett a communications magnate, purchased Vail in 1985 and immediately launched a series of improvements to shore up the parapets against the advances of increasingly bellicose neighbors. But even this strategic move was not made without reservations.

"Capital expenditure simply to take skiers from other resorts cannot be considered an efficient investment," Gillett said. "Nor can cutting prices for the same purpose. In either case, the advantage is lost when the competition responds in kind. Then all we accomplish is to spend great sums of money just to swap customers back and forth. Expansion makes good sense only when it is done to meet a skier demand."

Gillett believes such expenditure should be directed toward making

▶ *Strong winter winds attract ice boaters to this deep-frozen lake near Georgetown.*

ROBERT PITZER/AMWEST

resorts "guest friendly," creating an atmosphere that attracts uncommitted people to skiing through a broad range of activities and services.

"Some might view this as a problem, but I see it as an opportunity."

It is significant that these same thoughts are echoed by Seibert, who left Vail after 17 years as its driving force and now is back in the valley that he, more than anyone else, developed.

"We must maximize all forms of entertainment as a means of assuaging boredom during that time not spent on the slopes," Seibert said. "Ski resorts should be an attractive place to be, whether a person skis or not."

Vail's chairmen, the first and the latest, both emphasize the need to streamline transportation, to improve equipment, and to eliminate every other thing which might be perceived as a barrier to enjoyment. Such logic is altogether consistent with the surveys which tell us that skiing has evolved from a rugged, outdoor experience to a relatively manicured endeavor whose median participants are well into middle age. In Colorado, the average adult ski tourist is 39 years old with children, but the mass also includes a growing number of affluent single women. All seek much the same quality of experience, with equal parts comfort, variety, and excitement.

But Colorado skiing also has another focus, a substantial and highly active resident ski population centered in the metropolitan areas along the Front Range. These local skiers tend to be younger, more inclined toward excitement than ease, and foremost, keenly price conscious. Further, they are perceived, by their very numbers and

► *At Keystone, you can ski 13 hours a day on the most extensively lighted mountain in the West. Or, you may choose a variety of lift tickets for different times of day, left and middle.* JEFF ANDREW/KEYSTONE RESORT

► *For generations of skiers, the Hotel Jerome Bar, right, has been Aspen's favorite watering hole.* CHARLIE MEYERS

propensity to ski often, to hold the balance between success and failure when it comes to the all-important body count at season's end. How the resorts, particularly those close to Denver which attract the bulk of these residents, handle this balancing act without overindulging in competitive expansion and pricing is a primary key to their fiscal well-being.

Meanwhile, the cost of skiing inevitably is spurred ever higher by these same capital improvements and such ancillary factors as soaring liability insurance rates. The ultimate irony is that while some skiers may be attracted with more efficient lifts and new terrain, an equal number may be driven away by higher prices. Many observers are concerned that skiing increasingly is becoming a more luxurious and costly endeavor practiced by fewer people. Such a drift doubtlessly has precipitated the demise of numerous smaller areas, and some experts believe that some form of bankruptcy, with reorganization under the aegis of a larger company, is in the future of some major resorts as well.

Indeed, even in the best of times, ski-area ownership has become a corporate affair. Those old rough-and-ready pioneers who cut their own trails and strung their own lifts in an era when attorneys came to ski resorts only to ski have given way to managers with soft hands and, likely as not, law degrees.

But trend is not necessarily destiny. It well may be that this same old adventurous spirit still is alive, just jaunting off in a new direction and not quite as easily recognized inside a Brooks Brothers suit.

Behind these few dark clouds, skiing's horizons are bright with things new and exciting. Nowhere are they more radiant than in Colorado, where the trail still leads to the stars. ■

High, wild, and free

The ridge buckles and bends against the horizon as it slides past the window, a twisted tapestry of white beneath a bell jar of blue. Below this rambling crest, great snow basins take shape between granite spires to form billowy oceans of powder the texture of a lightly rumpled satin sheet. The analogy is more than coincidental. Those who have experienced both swear that backcountry powder skiing is better than sex.

The Jet Ranger helicopter slips past a series of fluted rock chimneys, climbs over the lip of a freshly formed cornice, circles once, and alights like a noisy hummingbird on a barren knob blown almost clean by an omnipresent wind.

Doors fly open, spilling brightly clad skiers. The chopper roars again, clatters aloft in a blast of snow crystals, and is gone in a twinkling. Only then do skiers scramble to their feet, gather up their gear, and drink in the delicious panorama. This tenuous perch is a long saddle on Treasury Ridge, midway between Treasury Mountain in the southeast and Treasure Mountain in the opposite direction.

Off in the distance to the south and east is a ski resort, Crested Butte. Somewhere beyond the twists and turns of the big basin that stretches out before the skiers is the little town of Marble, nestled in the upper reaches of the Crystal River valley beneath the monolith of Whitehouse Mountain. In between lies powder-skiing heaven.

It is axiomatic that there are no bad views in the grand world of helicopter skiing. This is one of the best. To the northeast, so

close it seems they may be touched by a ski pole, are the Maroon Bells. Straight across the valley are two more 14,000-foot peaks. Unwittingly, the old miners gave a weather report in their place names for this high, wild country: Siberia Lake, North Pole Basin, Frigid Air Pass. No matter. One man's hardship is another's powder.

There is a terrible, wonderful isolation to it all. The quiet is deafening. Someone shouts, a long, haunting "Hallooo" that rolls quickly down the slope and is just as suddenly swallowed up like a water droplet on hot sand. Four skiers stand unmoving, staring down at the wonder of it all, reluctant to initiate any blemish on nature's masterpiece.

The spell is broken by a skier bearing a bulky pack, who plunges off over the rim and, with a surgeon's skill, slices off the edge of a cornice which had begun to form over the upper run. There is no snowslide, an encouraging sign that the snowpack is stable and resistant to avalanche. Still, the group will take no chances. The route of descent has been selected to avoid dangerous slopes; around each neck is a homing device to facilitate rapid recovery should anyone be buried under snow.

Others follow with unbounded delight, throwing small rooster tails of snow, poetry on skis. Snow dancing, for those who do it well, is

DANN COFFEY/THE STOCK BROKER

a thing of consummate beauty. It is an experience that is both infrequent and fleeting on mountains where there are chair lifts, and there is little wonder that those who love it best are so willing to take the trouble and risks of the backcountry.

Beneath this upper basin, the slope funnels into a steeper pitch, then opens into a broader snowfield marked by giant hummocks which cast eerie shadows, forming dark tongues on glistening snow. As if by some unseen signal, all four skiers stop to admire their tracks, the personalized signatures of this uncommon enterprise. After a snowfall they will be gone, clearing the slate for the next author.

This open expanse gives way to timberline, where weathered evergreens cling to a tenuous existence and lend a ragged definition to the barren snowscape. Farther on, the trees grow taller and more dense, and suddenly, the helicopter appears on a bare knoll.

A few more turns and it is over, like those lovely dreams which end too soon. Always too soon.

The Bob and Willy show—a rivalry that made skiing richer

Seldom have two men shown such differences in the same pursuit. One is the product of wartime Germany, the other peacetime New Hampshire. One commands with an authority which spits thunderbolts, the other with dogged persuasiveness. One has been a consort of presidents and kings; the other hobnobs with network executives and movie stars.

Under different circumstances, Willy Schaeffler and Bob Beattie might have been fast friends. Both possess immense competitive instincts which unflaggingly have been directed toward the betterment of skiing in the United States. Both have waged a form of holy war against European dominance of the sport and, more than anyone else, have given American skiing the credibility it enjoys today. Both make their headquarters in Colorado—Schaeffler in Denver and Beattie in Aspen—and never fail to call attention to the superior quality of the skiing or to direct major international events to the state.

But fate cast them as oppo-nents early on, and this they have remained for more than two decades. They have been friends infrequently, allies occasionally, rivals always.

The competition began in 1956 with the arrival of Beattie, brash and combative, on the University of Colorado (CU) campus at Boulder to coach a ski team which, for all practical purposes, did not exist. Just 35 miles to the south at the University of Denver, Schaeffler's team already had won two national collegiate ski championships. Battle lines were drawn and weapons chosen carefully.

From the beginning, the conflict was as much over style as substance. Capitalizing on a dearth of American talent for nordic events, Schaeffler imported a procession of Norwegian students, strong young cross-country skiers and ski jumpers steeled by the intensely competitive fires of the homeland. Beattie countered with American-grown alpinists. The clashes between the nationalities and the coaches always were heated, sometimes rancorous.

For a time, Schaeffler's foreign legions won with monotonous regularity, claiming four NCAA championships from 1954 to 1957. It wasn't until Schaeffler took a two-year leave of absence to serve as director of all ski events for the 1960 Squaw Valley Olympics that Beattie's Colorado team broke through with consecutive championships in 1959 and 1960.

By now, Beattie had gathered the best young skiers in the nation into his stable: Buddy Werner, Billy Kidd, Jim Heuga, Bill Marolt, Chuck Ferries, Gordy Eaton, and Moose Barrows. When he also was given the job of U.S. Alpine Coach in 1961, the CU team and the national team were virtually the same. Beattie lambasted Schaeffler for importing Europeans for positions that could have been used to develop U.S. talent. Schaeffler fired back charges that Beattie used his position as national coach to help his recruiting at the university.

Their fortunes now had grown on a grander scale. Schaeffler had earned the world spotlight while performing the logistical magic that salvaged the Olympics; Beattie now vaulted to international prominence as a coach.

Always a battler, Beattie immediately took on the European establishment in disputes over what he felt were unfair starting positions for his lesser-known Americans. After years of frustration, his breakthrough finally came at the 1964 Innsbruck Olympics, where Kidd flashed to the silver medal in the slalom and Heuga followed with the bronze, the first alpine medals ever for U.S. men.

Beattie continued as coach and alpine program director through the 1968 Olympics, for a time operating the team from a tiny room tucked away in a corner of the Denver airport, then resigned to revive professional racing under the banner of World Pro Skiing. In 1981, he severed ties with the pro tour to concentrate on other aspects of his Aspen-based ski endeavors, including an expanding role as a national sportscaster.

Schaeffler, who had become a fixture as an official at international ski events following his magic at Squaw Valley, reached a zenith in the early seventies. But such a leap through time would neglect what may be the most dramatic moments in a life that has exceeded its share. A promising young racer in his native Bavaria, he suddenly found his career interrupted by war. Because his father opposed Adolph Hitler, young Schaeffler was placed in a penal battalion and shipped to the Russian front. He was wounded several times, once by a burst of shrapnel that lodged near his heart and years later caused him to undergo open-heart surgery four times. Captured by the Russians, he escaped and joined the Bavarian underground.

After the war, he taught skiing to American troops at Garmisch, where an early pupil was General George Patton. He came to the United States in 1948 in the hold of a bunk-to-bunk liberty ship. Penniless, he made his way to Denver, where he discovered that ski pioneer Larry

Jump was attempting to build the ski area which now is Arapahoe Basin. With an axe and a lone draft horse, Schaeffler cleared the mountain almost single-handedly for a salary of $45 per month. That October, when early snow halted the work, he learned that the University of Denver needed a ski coach. Just six months in the country with little command of the language, he convinced university officials to give him the job for what seemed a princely sum of $2,000 per year.

Not only did he win 13 NCAA titles in 15 years, finishing second the other times, but he also was directly responsible for having skiing accepted as a championship event. After his final national title in 1970, he was named coach of the U.S. Alpine Team and in 1972 watched his skiers win gold and bronze medals at the Olympics, the first such wins since 1964.

In failing health following the successive heart surgeries, Schaeffler still remained active in international ski circles, steadfastly maintaining his Denver residence despite medical advice to move to a lower elevation.

Both Schaeffler and Beattie have been given all the awards, all the accolades the sport has to offer. Somehow it doesn't seem enough.

▶ *Sun Up Bowl is just one of the massive snowfields that make up the famed Back Bowls of Vail.* DAVID LOKEY/ VAIL-BEAVER CREEK

About the author

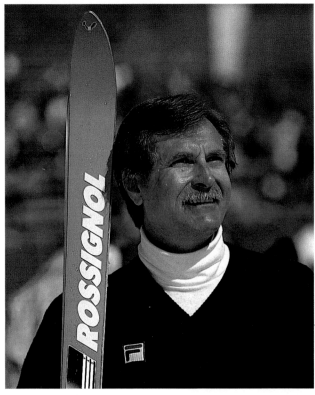

ANNE W. KRAUSE

Long before great waves of skiers began streaming up out of the Sun Belt bound for Colorado's high country, Charlie Meyers made the move in a big way. When he left his native Louisiana in 1966 to join the staff of the *Denver Post,* he never before had seen a ski and he'd seen very little snow. But since becoming ski editor of the newspaper a year later, his still-flowering romance with the sport has taken him across four continents and to as many Olympic games.

Over the years he has written about virtually every aspect of skiing and is the author of another book and more than 300 magazine articles, principally as a contributing editor to *Ski* magazine. He is a four-time recipient of the Harold Hirsch Award as the nation's leading ski writer and is the 1986 winner of the Lowell Thomas Award for excellence in ski journalism.

Through it all, he has maintained a particularly close attachment to his adopted Colorado, which during the same period, has evolved as the nation's leading ski center. His home in Boulder is at the head of a cross-country ski trail that leads into the foothills of the Rockies.

For more information

Arapahoe Basin
See Keystone Resort.

Aspen Highlands
P.O. Box T
Aspen, CO 81612
(303) 925-5300

Aspen Skiing Company
P.O. Box 1248
Aspen, CO 81612
(303) 925-1220

Beaver Creek
See Vail Associates, Inc.

Berthoud Pass
P.O. Box 3220
Idaho Springs, CO 80452
(303) 572-8014

Breckenridge Ski Area
P.O. Box 1058
Breckenridge, CO 80424
(303) 453-2368

Conquistador
P.O. Box 347
Westcliffe, CO 81252
(303) 783-9206

Copper Mountain Resort
P.O. Box 3001
Copper Mountain, CO 80443
(303) 968-2882

Crested Butte Mountain Resort
P.O. Box A
Mt. Crested Butte, CO 81224
(303) 349-2281

Cuchara Valley Resort
Resort Box 3
Cuchara, CO 81055
(303) 742-3163

Eldora
P.O. Box 430
Nederland, CO 80466
(303) 447-8013

Keystone Resort
P.O. Box 38
Keystone, CO 80435
(303) 468-2316

Loveland Basin Ski Area
P.O. Box 899
Georgetown, CO 80444
(303) 569-2288

Monarch Ski Resort
U.S. Highway 50
Garfield, CO 81227
(303) 539-2581

Powderhorn
P.O. Box 370
Mesa, CO 81643
(303) 268-5812

Purgatory
Durango Ski Corp.
P.O. Box 666
Durango, CO 81302
(303) 247-9000

St. Mary's Glacier
c/o Imports International
11975 East 40 Avenue
Denver, CO 80239
(303) 567-2582

SilverCreek
P.O. Box 4001
Silver Creek, CO 80446
(303) 887-3356

Ski Broadmoor
Colorado Springs, CO 80906
(303) 578-6027

Ski Cooper
P.O. Box 896
Leadville, CO 80461
(303) 486-3684

Ski Estes Park
P.O. Box 1379
Estes Park, CO 80517
(303) 586-4887

Ski Sunlight
10901 County Road 117
Glenwood Springs, CO 81601
(303) 945-7491

Snowmass Resort Association
P.O. Box 5566
Snowmass Village, CO 81615
(303) 923-2000

Steamboat Ski Corporation
2305 Mt. Werner Circle
Steamboat Springs, CO 80487
(303) 879-6111

Telluride Ski Resort
P.O. Box 307
Telluride, CO 81435
(303) 728-3856

Vail Associates, Inc.
P.O. Box 7
Vail, CO 81658
(303) 476-5601
Beaver Creek: (303) 949-5750

Winter Park Resort
P.O. Box 36
Winter Park, CO 80482
(303) 726-5514

Wolf Creek Ski Area
P.O. Box 1036
Pagosa Springs, CO 81147
(303) 264-2533

Colorado Ski Country USA
1410 Grant Street, Suite A-201
Denver, CO 80203
(303) 837-0793

Ski the Summit
P.O. Box 267
Dillon, CO 80435
(303) 468-6607

Also available in the Colorado Geographic Series . . .

The Rivers of Colorado   by Jeff Rennicke

Book One of the Colorado Geographic Series tells the story of Colorado's 100 magnificent rivers in 111 full-color photographs, maps, diagrams, charts, and a text filled with facts and amusing historical anecdotes. Gold-medal trout streams, the serene beauty of a slickwater river, roaring white water—the world of Colorado's rivers will fascinate you.

112 pages, 11" x 8 1/2", $14.95 softcover, $24.95 hardcover.

Colorado Mountain Ranges   by Jeff Rennicke

Dazzling color photographs of mountain peaks, wildlife, and wildflowers are the hallmark of Book Two in the Colorado Geographic Series. The geology that made Colorado's mountains possible, the natural history that brings them to life, and the recreation that makes them so much fun are presented in 135 color photos and an informative text.

128 pages, 11" x 8 1/2", $14.95 softcover, $24.95 hardcover.

Pikes Peak Country   by Jim Scott

From cosmopolitan Colorado Springs to the amazing Florissant fossil beds, Book Three explores the unique area around Pikes Peak in a lively text and 150 color photos. Covering geology, natural history, human history, and modern life, *Pikes Peak Country* adds another dimension to the Colorado Geographic Series.

104 pages, 11" x 8 1/2", $14.95 softcover, $24.95 hardcover.

Coming soon . . .

Colorado Parklands

Discover the beauty and excitement of Colorado's cherished parks—including Rocky Mountain, Mesa Verde, Black Canyon of the Gunnison, Dinosaur, Royal Gorge, Garden of the Gods, Great Sand Dunes, and many more—in Book Five of the Colorado Geographic Series. With color photos, maps, and graphics, *Colorado Parklands* interprets the geological, ecological, archaeological, and recreational resources that are Colorado's natural heritage.

To order . . .

The Rivers of Colorado, Colorado Mountain Ranges, Pikes Peak Country, Colorado Ski Country, Colorado Parklands

Call toll-free—1-800-582-BOOK—to order with Visa or Mastercard. Or send a check or money order and include $1.50 postage and handling for each book to Falcon Press, P.O. Box 279, Billings, MT 59103. (OUR GUARANTEE: If you are dissatisfied with any book obtained from Falcon Press, simply return your purchase for a full refund.)